IMAGES
of America

VINTONDALE

Eliza Furnace, the first vestige of industrial development in the Vintondale, has survived relatively untouched since 1845. Today it is the main focal point on the Ghost Town Trail. (Courtesy of the Dusza family collection.)

On the cover: Vintondale is seen here in 1906. This print was taken from a series of glass negatives that documented the construction of the Vinton Colliery Company's No. 6 mine. Taken from the vantage point of Plank Road, it shows the miners' houses on lower Maple Street. The main section of Vintondale is in the background. The glass negatives were donated by the Huth family to the archives of the Pennsylvania Historical and Museum Commission. (Denise Weber Collection, Pennsylvania Historical and Museum Archives.)

IMAGES
of America

VINTONDALE

Denise Dusza Weber

ARCADIA
PUBLISHING

Published by Arcadia Publishing
Charleston SC, Chicago IL, Portsmouth NH, San Francisco CA

Library of Congress Catalog Card Number: 2007932666

For all general information contact Arcadia Publishing at:
Telephone 843-853-2070
Fax 843-853-0044
E-mail sales@arcadiapublishing.com
For customer service and orders:
Toll-Free 1-888-313-2665

Visit us on the Internet at www.arcadiapublishing.com

*To all past and present residents of Vintondale, thank you
for sharing your experiences and photographs with me as I have
researched the history of this unique company town.*

CONTENTS

ACKNOWLEDGMENTS

This volume was compiled to celebrate Vintondale's 100th anniversary as a borough and to give past and present residents a photograph memory of their very special hometown. Many thanks go to Dr. Theresa McDevitt, Indiana University of Pennsylvania archivist, who put me in touch with Arcadia Publishing. McDevitt and her mother, Betty, also provided some very crucial photographs of early Vintondale. Others providing materials included Diane Dusza, Jean Hammer, Aileen Michelbacher-Ure, Fred Michelbacher, Albert Beres, John Bugal, Edward Hagens, Judy Morey Minzer, Amy Morey Gorman, Albert Pisaneschi, Charles Sago, Inez Biondo Soorus, George Lantzy, Robert Cresswell, Clarence Stephenson, Charles Hower, Henry Wehrum IV, Joanne Vasilko, Fr. Donald Dusza, Raymond Pioli, Claire Sebulsky, Estelle Wojtowicz, James MacFarlane, Margaret Schmidt, Mary Ellen Pytash, Leona Dusza, Clair Bearer, Walter and Barbara Pluchinsky, Lloyd Williams, Mary Martin, Beulah Bracken, and the Vintondale Homecoming Committee. Very special thanks go to Harold Swanson, who loaned his personally-developed photographs from the 1940s and the 1950s. Credit also goes to Mainline Publications for the use of 1977 flood photographs from the *Nanty Glo Journal*, the United Mine Workers of America for the use of the 1940 band photograph, and to the Johnstown *Tribune Democrat* for the use of 1940 bankruptcy photographs. Thank you to Linda Ries of the Pennsylvania Historical and Museum Commission archives for her advice and for obtaining permission to use the glass negative prints. Kudos also goes to Erin Vosgien, editor at Arcadia Publishing, for her continued support and encouragement. Publication of this volume is due to the largesse of Margaret Huth Schmidt.

INTRODUCTION

The borough of Vintondale was incorporated on September 4, 1907, but its origins go back to 1890. In that year, Judge Augustine Vinton Barker began purchasing land and coal rights in the area of the forks of the Blacklick Creek. Barker was preceded by David Ritter, who 50 years earlier built the Eliza Furnace. The furnace was a failure, and the valley was basically abandoned until 1890.

Barker was able to attract eastern investors for his purchases, including Warren Delano III, maternal uncle of Franklin Delano Roosevelt. Ground for the new village, eventually named for Barker, was broken on July 19, 1893. By 1894, lots were up for sale through the Blacklick Land and Improvement Company. Many lots were purchased by the Barker brothers and the Thomas Griffith family, both of whom had sawmills in Vintondale. Barker was instrumental in having a branch of the Pennsylvania Railroad constructed as far as Vintondale.

The Vinton Colliery Company shipped out the first coal from the No. 1 mine in October 1894. The first superintendent of mines for Vinton Colliery was Clarence R. Claghorn, who introduced a modified long wall system at No. 3 when it opened in 1899. In 1901, a newly organized coal company, the Lackawanna Coal and Coke Company, purchased Nos. 1 and 2 and proceeded to build two large mine complexes at Wehrum and at Lackawanna No. 3. In 1905, Delano repurchased Nos. 1 and 2. He wanted to prove that he could profitably produce coke in Vintondale. The large flood plain on the north side of the Blacklick Creek, originally laid out in lots, became a beehive of activity in 1906. Hundreds of laborers, bricklayers, and carpenters were employed to build the tipple, washery, powerhouse, machine shop, ammonia plant, and a battery of 152 beehive coke ovens.

Skilled and unskilled laborers poured into Vintondale from the surrounding counties, the hard-coal region, and southern and eastern Europe. Over 25 languages were spoken in Vintondale in the 1920s, as verified by the 1920 census. The company built a large, imposing stone building on Second and Main Streets to house the company office and the company store. The Vinton Colliery Company, adamantly antiunion, forced the miners to purchase their food at its store. This antiunion mind set assisted Vintondale in earning its reputation as a "wild and woolly" mining town. Company coal and iron police patrolled the town and met every train to see who was coming into town.

Numerous businesses catered to farmers and the ethnic groups. There were at least 30 businesses open in the 1920s, including a jewelry store, three clothing stores, two meat markets, six grocery stores, a confectionery, two garages, and an undertaking and paint store. Vintondale had two different wholesale liquor distributors between 1895 and 1920 when Prohibition took affect. Vintondale miners were not going to do without their beer and whiskey, so many wives began to make moonshine, the best coming from a still up on Chickaree Hill.

The company was the main beneficiary of the borough incorporation. Company officials dominated the borough council. Louis Burr, company engineer and son of the company treasurer, served from 1906 to 1911. Otto "Pappy" Hoffman, superintendent of mines, was council president from 1915 to 1930. Town merchants tried to break this lock on power in 1913 and 1915 by passing petitions to open council positions to non-company men.

Vintondale first reached national attention during the 1922 coal strike. The company positioned guardhouses that were manned with searchlights at every entrance into town. Heavily armed mounted coal and iron police patrolled the streets. The fledgling American Civil Liberties Union sent Arthur Garfield Hayes to investigate the plight of the miners. He was promptly arrested for trespassing on company property–the sidewalk. The company men initiated a walkout in 1924 over a wage cut. Many were members of the Ku Klux Klan, and a cross was burned on No. 6 hill. Known as the Ku Klux Klan strike, the company evicted the agitators and resumed its control over the town.

The company's hand was in all aspects of life in Vintondale. It controlled the entertainment, including picnics, the movie theater, and the baseball team. Not even the school board could escape the controlling hand of the company. In the 1920s, the superintendent's wife was president of the school board. In spite of its notorious reputation, the company was interested in education. As the town expanded, new schools were constructed. The first four-year high school opened in 1927, and many Vintondale students went on to distinguished careers in teaching, business, and the medical fields.

Ironically, Vintondale's miners were legally permitted to unionize during the Roosevelt administration. Between 400 and 500 miners had belonged to United Mine Workers of America (UMWA) Local 621, but it was disbanded in 1973 for lack of membership. Vintondale barely survived the Great Depression. Work was very sporadic, sometimes only two days a month. In March 1940, Vintondale again made national headlines when the company shut down the mine and company store without any notice. The local worked with District Two and national UMWA leaders and with Warren Delano's brother Frederic to reorganize the company. The Vinton Coal and Coke Company emerged from one of the first Chapter 11 bankruptcies in Pennsylvania.

During World War II, the company was hard-pressed to keep up production for the war due to the lack of miners. In December 1945, coke production ceased when the washery burned to the ground. Following World War II, many families moved out, searching for better jobs. The No. 1 mine closed in 1948, but even then there were 248 union employees at No. 6. Following the premature death of Clarence Schwerin II in 1957, his sons sold the mine to Tony Collins. The mine went bankrupt again and was purchased by Johnstown Coal and Coke Company and then Driscoll Coal Company. The final year of production was in 1968. The mine flat was abandoned and in the 1970s the usable coal in the rock dumps on the No. 6 flat was recycled by the United States Soil Conservation Service. The 1977 Johnstown flood washed out three bridges on the Pennsylvania Railroad and the Cambria and Indiana Railroad, ending 84 years of railroading in the middle Blacklick Valley. In 1994, the former roadbed became the Ghost Town Trail, a rail trail. The No. 6 flat was converted into a passive acid mine drainage system between 1995 and 2005 by the AMD&ART (acid mine drainage and art) project.

Vintondale has passed through many stages in its history, from an industrial giant, to a hotbed of labor unrest, to a retirement village. Today for the first time in its troubled history, Vintondale finally has clean drinking water and a sewage system, but no schools or grocery stores.

One

EARLY INDUSTRIES

Eliza Furnace, the showpiece of the Ghost Town Trail, was built of hand-hewn stones in 1845 by David Ritter and George Rodgers. A failure from the start, it shut down by 1847. Local iron ore was of low quality, shipping costs were prohibitive, and the main line of the Pennsylvania Railroad did not follow the Blacklick Creek as hoped. Many legends have arisen about Eliza Furnace, but most are untrue. Ritter did not hang himself in front of the furnace; he actually died in Catawissa, Columbia County, in 1858. His new partner, Lot Irvin, did hang himself at an iron furnace in Greenville.

Eliza Furnace's heat exchanger on top was the latest technology in the 1840s, but it only raised the temperature of the cold blast a few degrees. Sold at sheriff's sale in 1849, the property passed through a series of owners. Eventually the Driscoll Coal Company deeded it to the Cambria County History Society in 1965.

Large lumber companies moved in to exploit the timber in the 1890s. The Griffiths and the Barkers from Ebensburg operated sawmills. The largest mill belonged to the Vinton Lumber Company, a subsidiary of the Clearfield Lumber Company. After timbering the north branch of the Blacklick Creek, the Vinton Lumber Company moved to Kentucky. It sold its Blacklick and Yellow Creek Railroad to the Coleman-Weaver coal interests. The railroad became the Cambria and Indiana Railroad, which operated until 1995.

Coal and coke from the Vintondale mines were hauled out on the Cambria and Clearfield branch of the Pennsylvania Railroad. The line was completed to Vintondale in 1894 and to Blacklick in Indiana County in 1903. The line was abandoned after the 1977 flood. Today the rail bed has been converted into the very popular Ghost Town Trail.

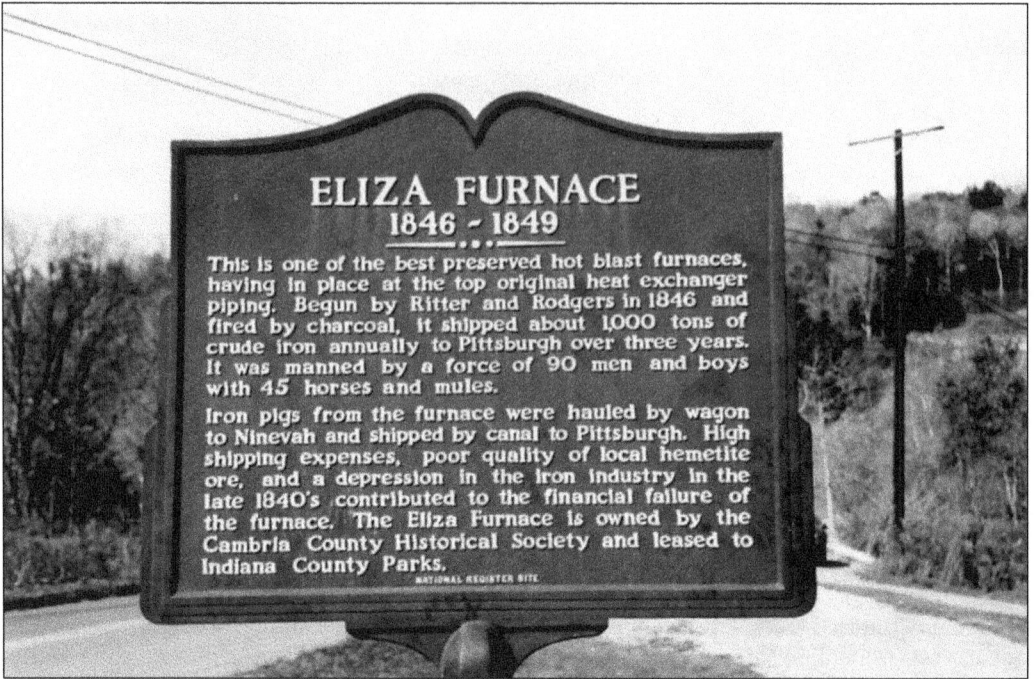

The Eliza Furnace historical marker, along with other interpretive signage, was installed at the Eliza Furnace site by the Indiana County Parks and Trails. (Courtesy of Charles Hower.)

Amanda "Peg" Arble, a clerk in the Vintondale Supply Company, Ltd. store, poses in front of the Eliza Furnace. The two-story building in the background may have been an office or a boardinghouse for the ironworkers. Around 1900, it was used as a schoolhouse and then converted to housing for the coal miners before being dismantled in the 1930s. (Courtesy of Betty and Theresa McDevitt.)

Eliza Furnace's pipes on the top were heat exchangers, the newest innovation in the 1840s. In 1994, the Indiana County Parks and Trails signed a 99-year lease with the Cambria County Historical Society to maintain the furnace site. Gates have been installed at the furnace openings to prevent people from climbing inside. This photograph was taken in 1966. (Courtesy of Denise Weber.)

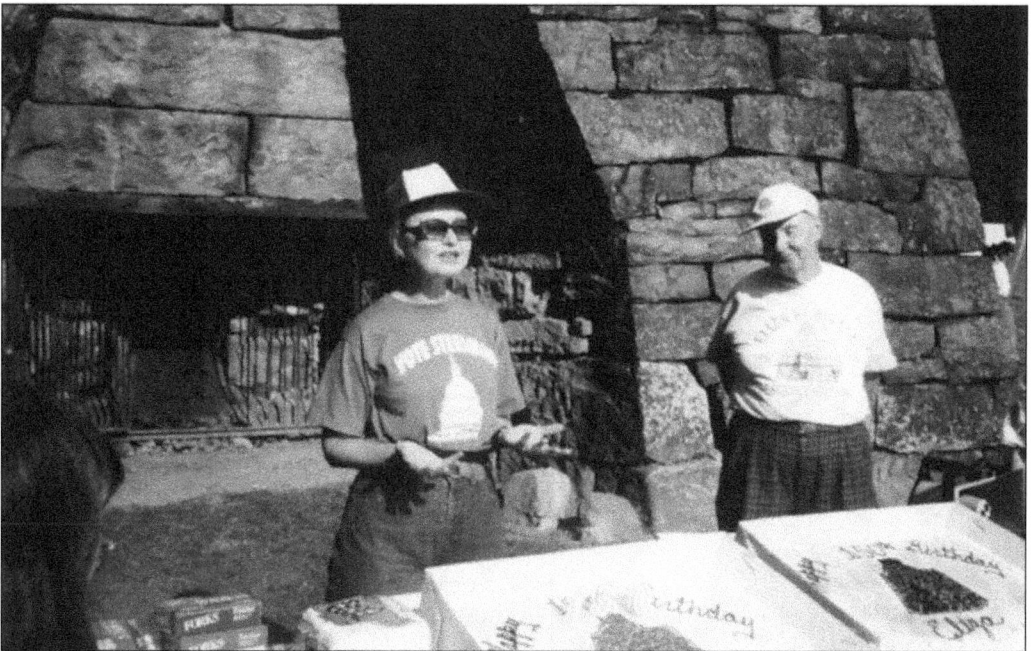

Eliza Furnace celebrated its 150th birthday in 1996. Cutting the birthday cake were state representative Sara Steelman and Lew Ripley, president of the Cambria County Historical Society. Ripley's ancestors, the Gillins of Vinco, helped construct the furnace. (Courtesy of Denise Weber.)

The Vinton Lumber Company mill was located in Rexis, across the north branch of the Blacklick Creek from Eliza Furnace. It was one of the largest mills in the eastern United States. William Clarkson is seated on a pile of lumber. Mary Lynch, his future wife, is on the far left. (Courtesy of Leona Clarkson Dusza.)

A single-lane iron bridge connected Vintondale and Rexis. The bridge is mentioned in local author Jack Burgan's novel *Martin Butterfield*. Photographed on the bridge are Lloyd Arbogast, company controller, and his fiancée Amanda "Peg" Arble. (Courtesy of Betty and Theresa McDevitt.)

The iron bridge was a hazard, and Indiana County replaced it in 1960 with a concrete bridge. Seen in the photograph are the old bridge and the new one under construction. (Courtesy of Diane Dusza.)

The concrete arch bridge near the train station was replaced after the 1977 flood. Debris had backed up behind the bridge, and the high water caused severe damage to the houses on Main Street between Sixth Street and the bridge. The contractor had to resort to dynamiting the old bridge to remove it. (Courtesy of Denise Weber.)

The Pennsylvania Railroad hauled out the first Vintondale coal in 1894 and continued pulling the cars laden with black diamonds until 1977. This train, nicknamed the "Mountain Goat," provided passenger service between Indiana and Cresson and stopped in Vintondale twice daily in each direction until 1931. The Buffalo, Rochester and Pittsburgh Railway (BR&P) negotiated trackage rights on the Ebensburg and Blacklick branch as far as Vintondale. The BR&P hauled coal and coke to Buffalo, New York. (Courtesy of Clair Bearer.)

The Cambria and Indiana Railroad hauled coal from Colver to Rexis, where it was picked up by the Pennsylvania Railroad. In 1924, the train was robbed of a payroll meant for the Colver mine. The thieves were caught, but the payroll was never found. Eventually the line changed from a steam engine to a battery-powered hoodlebug. Passenger service ended in 1931, and coal haulage ceased after the 1977 flood washed away the Red Mill Bridge. (Courtesy of George Lantzy.)

Vintondale had separate passenger and freight stations. Passenger service ended in 1931, and the freight station was torn down in the 1960s. (Courtesy of Leona Clarkson Dusza.)

Vinton Colliery Company used a narrow-gauge engine called a dinkey to shift supplies between its No. 1 and No. 6 mines. When the Lackawanna Coal and Coke Company owned No. 1 and No. 2, a dinkey track was built from No. 1 to the Lackawanna No. 3 mine west of Vintondale. Driving the dinkey is Jim Dempsey. In the rear is Gordon "Flip" Thomas. Manning the switches is John Roberts. (Courtesy of Albert Pisaneschi.)

In 1991, Laurie LaFontaine, with support of Ed Patterson of Indiana County Parks and Recreation and Jerry Brant of Northern Cambria Community Development Corporation (NORCAM), sought funds to turn the abandoned rail line into the Ghost Town Trail. Kovalchick Salvage Company donated the right of way, enabling matching funds to be awarded. The rail bridge here in Vintondale was adapted for bicycle use. (Courtesy of Denise Weber.)

In 1994, the trail opened between Dilltown and Nanty Glo. Since then, three additional sections have been added. The missing link is the two bridges below Dilltown that were washed out in the 1977 flood. Through the efforts of Patterson, the Pennsylvania Conservation Corps constructed way stations in Vintondale and Dilltown. LaFontaine is seen here at the dedication of the Red Mill Bridge in 1999. (Courtesy of Denise Weber.)

Two

VINTON COLLIERY COMPANY'S MEN

Augustine Vinton Barker did not play a direct role in the running of the Vinton Colliery Company mines, but he was instrumental in obtaining land and mineral rights for the Vinton Colliery Company and the Lackawanna Coal and Coke Company. A photograph of Barker is not available. Barker was able to attract eastern investors who were interested in opening up the bituminous coal fields in Cambria County. This included Warren Delano III, who wanted to prove that the coal in the Blacklick Valley was suitable for coking. In 1894, the mines in his new town of Vintondale began shipping coal to eastern markets. In 1901, he sold No. 1 and No. 2 to Lackawanna Coal and Coke Company. In 1905, he repurchased the mines. He then set out to build a large mine complex, including 152 coke ovens, a washery, a powerhouse, and an ammonia plant on the north side of Blacklick Creek.

The first superintendent, Clarence R. Claghorn, introduced modified long wall mining at No. 3 and at the Wehrum mines. When an economic slowdown closed Wehrum in 1904 and 1905, Claghorn left for Washington State. The long wall method was abandoned because of its high expense. Claghorn returned briefly in 1917 when Vinton Colliery reopened the abandoned Claghorn mines on the lower Blacklick Creek.

Superintendents who made an impact on the town were Charles Hower, Otto Hoffman, and Milton Brandon. Not only were they to keep production at top level, but they were also expected to keep out the union.

Unionization came with the New Deal, and so did many changes in Vintondale. The company doctor left and the new doctor had the approval of the union. The coal and iron police were replaced by part-time policemen who were union members. Mining ended in 1968 and the No. 6 flat was cleaned up by the U.S. Soil Conservation Service. Between 1995 and 2005, treatment of the acid mine drainage changed the No. 6 flat into a recreation area.

Warren Delano III, maternal uncle of Pres. Franklin Delano Roosevelt, was born in 1852. Delano was a principal investor in the Vinton Colliery Company and the Lackawanna Coal and Coke Company. He repurchased the No. 1 and No. 2 mines and built the new No. 6 coking complex in 1905 and 1906. Delano died accidentally on September 9, 1920, when his horse bolted in front of a train in Barrytown, New York. (Courtesy of Clarence Stephenson.)

Henry Wehrum, general manager of the Lackawanna Steel Company of Scranton, was instrumental in moving the steel works to Lackawanna, New York. A subsidiary, the Lackawanna Coal and Coke Company opened a new mining town, named Wehrum, downstream from Vintondale. Economic downturns led to his dismissal in 1903. Wehrum retired to his home in Elmhurst where he died in 1905. (Courtesy of Henry Wehrum IV.)

Clarence R. Claghorn, first superintendent of the Vinton Colliery Company and the Lackawanna Coal and Coke Company, had worked in Birmingham, Alabama, and studied long wall mining in England. He introduced a modified long wall system at Vinton Colliery's No. 3 and at the Lackawanna mines. In 1903, Lackawanna opened a new mining town called Claghorn, which today is a ghost town. (Courtesy of Robert Cresswell.)

Clarence Schwerin Sr., a chemical engineer, was hired to improve the quality of the Vintondale coke. In 1914, he was appointed president of the Vinton Colliery Company. After the death of Delano in 1920, he was in charge of the whole operation. During the 1920s, Schwerin was instrumental in keeping out the union. He died in 1944. (Courtesy of Clarence Schwerin III.)

Charles Hower, hired as superintendent of the Vinton Colliery Company in 1906, was the first to move into the new superintendent's mansion. In 1909, he was dismissed because of a prolonged miners' strike. He was instrumental in rescuing miners hurt in the 1909 Wehrum mine explosion. The Hower family eventually settled in eastern Pennsylvania. (Courtesy of the Denise Weber Collection, Pennsylvania Historical and Museum Commission Archives.)

Otto Hoffman, known as "Pappy" or "King Otto," was hired as chief engineer in 1911 and became superintendent in 1915. Hoffman kept a tight rein for over 15 years until his tragic accidental death at the No. 6 tipple in March 1930. From left to right are unidentified, Harry Clark, Michael Grosik Sr., and Otto Hoffman. (Courtesy of the Huth family collection.)

Milton Brandon, superintendent at Graceton Coal and Coke, was appointed as superintendent after Hoffman's death. Brandon steered the company through the Great Depression, unionization, the 1940 bankruptcy and reorganization into Vinton Coal and Coke Company. Here Brandon is seen with his son Dr. Boyd Brandon and grandson Tom. (Courtesy of Dr. Boyd Brandon.)

Lloyd Arbogast was hired as chief clerk for the Vinton Colliery Company in 1912 and was promoted to comptroller in 1916. In his biography in a Cambria County history, Arbogast took credit for helping to establish Vintondale Borough. However, Vintondale was incorporated five years before his arrival. He served on the borough council and was a vice president of the Vintondale State Bank. (Courtesy of Betty and Theresa McDevitt.)

Lloyd Arbogast was engaged to Amanda "Peg" Arble, a clerk at the Vintondale Supply Company, Ltd. store. The engagement was broken, and Arble returned home to Carrolltown where she married her childhood sweetheart, Oliver Stoltz. Eventually Arbogast married a schoolteacher, and the couple lived in a suite of rooms at the Vintondale Inn. He left Vintondale in 1929 due to illness. (Courtesy of Betty and Theresa McDevitt.)

John Huth came from Frackville in 1906 as a chainboy on the engineering crew. He advanced to the position of mining engineer by taking correspondence courses with the International School in Scranton. Huth played on the company baseball team in his early years and later advanced to assistant superintendent. (Courtesy of Huth family collection.)

Clarence Schwerin Jr. took over operation of the Vinton Coal and Coke Company in 1944 after his father's death. Schwerin maintained a good working relationship with the unionized miners, but that ended with his premature death due to lung cancer in 1956. With safety-flame lamp in hand, Schwerin is preparing to make an inspection of the No. 6 mine. (Courtesy of Huth family collection.)

On the grounds of the superintendent's mansion were an apple orchard, a tennis court, and a grape arbor. Several peacocks roamed the yard. Ivan Dotts converted the carriage house, seen in the background, into living quarters in the late 1940s. (Courtesy of Aileen Ure and Fred Michelbacher.)

23

In 2001, Charles Hower III, grandson of Charles Hower, came to Vintondale searching for his roots. Almost 100 years after the previous image, Charles III and brother William pose for a photograph on the porch of the same mansion. (Courtesy of Denise Weber.)

This photograph was taken at the top of Third Street. Ss. Peter and Paul Russian Orthodox Church is at the top of the street. Behind the church is a community park where the new four-year high school was built in 1926 and 1927. Mainly company men lived in the houses above Griffith Street. Third Street consisted of company and privately-owned houses. (Courtesy of Albert Pisaneschi.)

Three

COAL MINING

Although preceded by iron manufacturing and lumbering, coal mining and coke making became the signature industries in Vintondale. At one time there were six mines operating in Vintondale. Vinton Colliery's No. 1 mine, located between Shuman Run and Second Street, operated between 1894 and 1948. Loaded one-ton cars came out of the drift and across a trestle to the tipple on the far side of Shuman Run. The coal was dumped into waiting hopper cars and pushed to the siding that paralleled Plank Road. No. 2 was a short-lived drift mine that was located southeast of Plank Road. The coal seams outcropped onto the sides of Chickaree Hill.

Clarence R. Claghorn introduced the long wall method at No. 3, which opened in 1899. The mine was near the "Big Curve" on Twin Rocks Road. Warren Delano III also operated eight experimental coke ovens at this mine. It closed in 1915. Several small operators mined it as a house coal mine until it was washed out by the 1977 flood.

No. 4 was located below Fourth Street, and its coal was eventually taken out by No. 1 and No. 6.

The Cambridge Bituminous Coal Company of Frackville opened No. 5, located halfway between Vintondale and Bracken. Its holdings became part of a lease between the Griffiths of Ebensburg and the Vinton Colliery Company. The only traces of the mine are a small bony pile on an island in the Blacklick Creek and a stone trestle wall.

No. 6 was constructed in 1906 and included a tipple, washery to wash the impurities from the coking coal, a battery of 152 stone-encased bee-hive ovens, a power plant that made direct current, a machine shop, and an ammonia plant that was to recycle the gasses given off by the coke ovens.

Vintondale's mines were not very profitable until the First World War. In 1917, Warren Delano III began an expansion program to build more houses for the miners on Chickaree Hill. He also reopened the mining town of Claghorn.

The No. 1 mine complex included the drift mouth, several outbuildings, and a trestle that crossed Shuman Run to the tipple. In this 1906 photograph, the mule barn is in the foreground, and the bony pile is directly behind the barn. The superintendent's yard abutted the mine. (Courtesy of the Denise Weber Collection, Pennsylvania State Historical Commission Archives.)

Loaded mine cars from No. 1 exited the drift mouth and crossed a large trestle to the tipple. There the coal was weighed and dumped into waiting hopper cars. (Courtesy of Lloyd Williams.)

The drift mouth of No. 1 was located between First Street extension and Chickaree Hill. The mine extended several miles into Chickaree Mountain toward Rager's Hollow. An air shaft was built on Rummel's farm. (Courtesy of Betty and Theresa McDevitt.)

Above the two couples is the No. 1 trestle. Empty hoppers were pushed up sidings that paralleled Shuman Run. The mule barn is the large building on the other side of the trestle. Tracks for the dinkey train are in the center of the photograph. (Courtesy of Betty and Theresa McDevitt.)

Waste rock and loose coal were discarded on bony pile, also known as a rock dump. The coal caught on fire by spontaneous combustion, and the rock dumps burned for years. A by-product were red-dog chunks of baked clay that were used for patching the ruts in the streets. More noxious results were the stench of rotten eggs and blue-colored smoke that covered the town. (Courtesy of Betty and Theresa McDevitt.)

In 1923 or 1924, there was excitement in Vintondale because an airplane passed over the borough at a low elevation. The pilot was taking aerial photographs of Vintondale. This Underwood and Underwood Aerial Division photograph shows the layout of the entire town, including the new houses on Chickaree Hill and the city block that made up the superintendent's house and yard. (Courtesy of the Huth and Morey families.)

Another Underwood and Underwood Aerial Division photograph shows the large No. 6 mine complex. The Blacklick Creek is at the bottom of the photograph. Several foot bridges cross the creek for the miners' use. The washery and powerhouse are in the center. Behind them is the battery of 152 coke ovens. The tipple is behind the washery, and the Pennsylvania Railroad tracks hug the edge of No. 6 hill. (Courtesy of the Huth family.)

Four of the Vinton Colliery Company's mines are seen in this Underwood and Underwood Aerial Division photograph. No. 1 is in the lower right corner. The rock dumps of No. 2 are in center right beside the railroad tracks. No. 3 is in the upper right, and No. 6 is in the center. The Vintondale Inn is center left. (Courtesy of the Huth family.)

In 1906, Vintondale was a beehive of activity. Dozens of carpenters, bricklayers, and laborers were building the new office and company store, the washery, the machine shop, power plant, ammonia plant, tipple, and the 152 coke ovens. The coal was washed to remove impurities that might damage the coke. (Courtesy of the Denise Weber Collection, Pennsylvania Historical Museum Commission Archives.)

Missing from this photograph are the water pipes that were needed to douse the coke and the lorry that loaded the ovens from the top. The ovens burned from 36 to 72 hours. (Courtesy of the Denise Weber Collection, Pennsylvania Historical and Museum Commission Archives.)

VINTON COLLIERY COKE OVENS, VINTONDALE, PA.

Coal went from the tipple to the washery. From there, washed coal traveled to the storage bin located over the ovens. From there the coal was loaded into the lorry. (Courtesy of Betty and Theresa McDevitt.)

The washery was a large, five story, brick-encased building that washed impurities from the coal that was used for coking. (Denise Weber Collection, Pennsylvania Historical and Museum Commission Archives.)

31

This postcard shows the washery and power plant before 1923. Untreated dirty water from the washery was dumped into the Blacklick Creek along with the acid drainage from the mines. (Courtesy of the Huth family collection.)

In 1923, the company built a new wooden coal bin to store washed coal for coking or making electricity. (Courtesy of Betty and Theresa McDevitt.)

Coal is being loaded on the left track under the No. 6 tipple. On the center track, a coke-drawing machine is loading coke into a coke rack. The lorry is located on top of the ovens. Next to the ovens is a pile of coke. The washery is on the right and the coke ovens have been charged. (Courtesy of the Huth family collection.)

A panorama of the No. 6 complex and the town is seen from Plank Road. Note the lack of trees on No. 6 hill. (Courtesy of Betty and Theresa McDevitt.)

Cows often roamed freely in town. Several pastures were used, such as Dancha's, which was located above Plank Road; the Mule Field at the western end of town; and the Green Grass above No. 1 mine. The houses are on lower Maple Street. (Courtesy of Betty and Theresa McDevitt.)

Loaded cars from No. 1 sat on the sidings paralleling Plank Road until the Pennsylvania Railroad picked up a trainload. The mines suffered from a chronic shortage of hoppers. Note that the loaded coal then was in large lumps. The powdery loose coal was dumped onto the bony piles. In the left center is First Street, and the No. 6 mine is not visible because of the pollution from the coke ovens. Notice the lack of grass and trees in the yards. (Courtesy of the Huth family collection.)

The No. 6 mine closed in 1968 after 62 years of mining. The mine was sealed, and the remaining out-buildings were salvaged for scrap. The rock dumps on the No. 6 flat were leveled, and the refuse sold to the power plants. The United States Soil Conservation Service, now NSCS, brought in topsoil and seeded and planted trees on the site. This March 1974 photograph shows the tipple and the machine shop ruins. (Courtesy of Diane Dusza.)

By October 1974, the tipple and most of the machine shop were gone. The foundation in the center of the photograph was the washery that burned in 1945. In front of the washery, small bony piles wait to be recycled. (Courtesy of Diane Dusza.)

By 1992, all traces of mining were gone from the No. 6 flat. The coke ovens were leveled, and the ground was covered with topsoil and seeded. (Courtesy of Diane Dusza.)

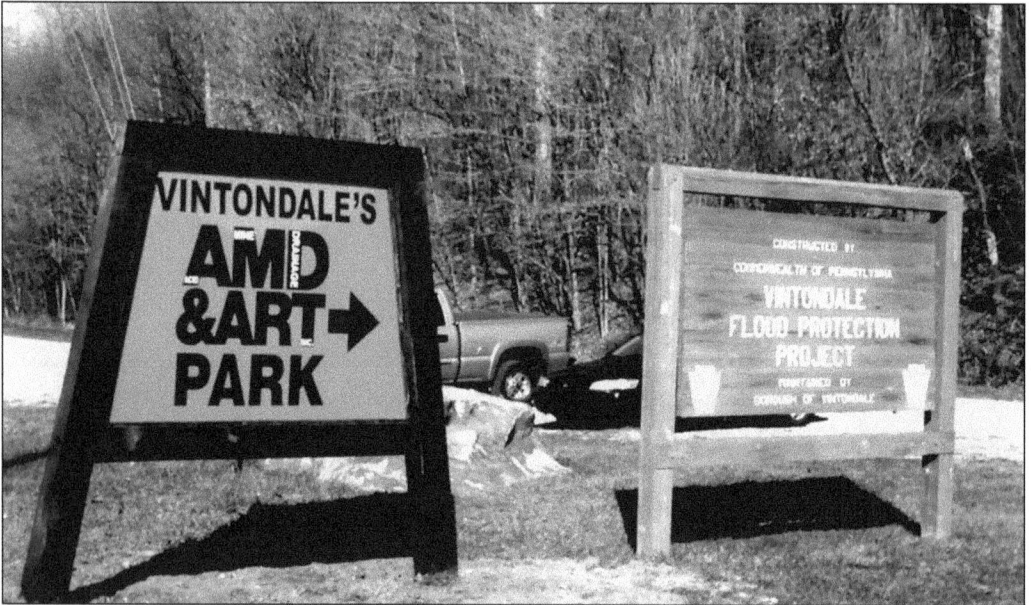

In the 1990s, two projects perked the interest of the now-quiet town of Vintondale. The long-awaited flood control dikes were finally constructed, and in 1995 discussions started on treating the acid mine drainage with passive treatment ponds. The AMD&ART project was completed in 2005. (Courtesy of Denise Weber.)

In 1992, 15 years after the 1977 flood, the flood-control project was completed. The Blacklick Creek was dredged, and the stone for the dike wall came from Rexis Hill. (Courtesy of Denise Weber.)

AMD&ART is a plan for passive treatment of mine acid drainage. The brainchild of Dr. Allen Comp, it was in the discussion stages when the state drilled three holes in the north branch of the Blacklick Creek to relieve the water pressure in the No. 6 mine. The sulfur water had been seeping into the homes in the lower end of town. The AMD&ART had to find a new source of acid mine drainage to treat. (Courtesy of Diane Dusza.)

In November 1994, AMD&ART unveiled the black marble slab that marks the portal of the No. 6 mine. On the slab is an etching showing Vintondale miners entering and leaving the mine. The caricatures were taken from a movie filmed in Vintondale during the Depression. (Courtesy of Denise Weber.)

Attending the dedication were three miners who had worked at No. 6. From left to right are Raymond Dodson, John Beres, and Steve Dusza. (Courtesy of Denise Weber.)

At the site of the former tipple, a mosaic map, modeled after a 1920s insurance map showing the location of the various mine buildings, was installed. Surrounding the map are polished black marble squares etched with early photographs of Vintondale. (Courtesy of Denise Weber.)

An AMD&ART History Symposium was held on July 8, 2005, to celebrate the grand opening of the project. Keynote speaker was Dr. Brent Glass, director of the Smithsonian National Museum of American History. Glass was recruited by Jeanie Gleason, a member of the AMD&ART board. (Courtesy of Denise Weber.)

In times of strife, the Vinton Colliery Company employed extra coal and iron police to patrol the town. In this early 1920s photograph the police, nicknamed the "pussyfoots" by the striking miners, are dressed in uniforms similar to those of the Pennsylvania State Constabulary. The officer in the center of the photograph is Jack Butala, chief of police. The names of the other officers are unknown. (Courtesy of the Huth family collection.)

Harry McArdle, Vintondale's second police officer, is surveying activity at the corner of Third and Main Streets. Behind him was Jacob Brett's general store and later Callet's wholesale liquor distributing company. In 1921, Philip Wayne opened an automobile repair shop and gas station in the building. Joe Hasen demolished the building and replaced it with a brick building that housed Hasen's Confectionery and the doctor's office. (Courtesy of Albert Pisaneschi.)

Four

UNIONIZATION
AND BANKRUPTCY

The Vinton Colliery Company, notoriously antiunion, took many harsh measures to keep out the United Mine Workers of America (UMWA). Guardhouses with mounted spotlights sat at each entrance to town. Heavily-armed company police patrolled the streets and met the trains. During the national coal strike in 1922, Vintondale miners did not walk out, and the fledgling American Civil Liberties Union sent Arthur Garfield Hayes to investigate the conditions in Vintondale. He was arrested for walking on company property. Hayes sued and lost his case. In 1924, Vintondale went on strike because of a wage cut. It was known as the Ku Klux Klan strike because many of the company men were Klan members. The majority of the strikers were evicted.

Ironically it was Warren Delano III's nephew, Pres. Franklin Delano Roosevelt, who brought the union to Vintondale. New Deal legislation legalized collective bargaining, and the Vinton Colliery Company could not stop the miners. However, they signed up on the Rexis side of the iron bridge. The new UMWA local was 621.

Significant changes resulted from unionization. James MacFarlane, the company doctor, resigned. The town police chief, the infamous Jack Butala, lost his job and moved to New York. The union miners paid $1 a day for a check-weighman who verified the correct weight of the loaded coal. The most significant change was political. In the next election, the town voted overwhelmingly Democratic and has ever since.

Vintondale again captured national attention when the Vinton Colliery Company shut down the mine and the company store without notice on March 14, 1940. The plight of the miners caught the attention of local and national newspapers. The Johnstown *Tribune Democrat* published a series of photographs in its March 19 issue. Local 621 president John Biondo organized patrols to guard company property. The union contract allowed a maintenance crew to keep the mine pumps going and to dig enough coal to keep the powerhouse in operation. Eventually a reorganization under Chapter 11 bankruptcy laws was completed. The Vinton Colliery Company became the Vinton Coal and Coke Company.

Vintondale's Local 621 band had the privilege of playing at the 50th annual UMWA convention in Cincinnati, Ohio, in January 1940. Band members were mainly miners or children of miners. The band leader was William Jendrick. Pictured from left to right are (first row) William Jendrick, George Wilson, Frank Funyak, Ross Ling, Tommy Rafas, George Sileck, Ralph Moore, Margaret Balko, David ?, Margaret Borczik, Margaret Farkas, Stephen Oblackovich, Andrew Beres, unidentified, George Vascovich, three unidentified, and band leader Michael Temnerelle of Beaverdale; (second row) unidentified, J. Nemetz, Joseph McGee, unidentified, John Checkan,

unidentified, Charles Gongloff, William Gasser, ? Ezo, and Charles Kerekish; (third row) Mario Ugoletti, William Hagens, Frank Scenna, Desmond Hallas, Emma Jane Daly, unidentified, Neal Feldman, and Albert Gongloff; (fourth row) unidentified, Benjie Giazzon, George Resinko, unidentified, Jospeh Lutsko, John Harnots, Victor Viga, and William Morris; (fifth row) John Martich, Andrew Grosik, Helen Sofko, William Wray, Alice Sileck, Lester Jansura, and three unidentified. (Courtesy of John Bugal and the United Mine Workers of America.)

The band proudly marched through Vintondale to the train station in the summer of 1939 or 1940. In the background are the Farkas Hotel, Cresswell Electric, and the Vinton Colliery Company store. The band broke up during World War II due to many of the musicians entering the service. (Courtesy of Albert Beres.)

This photograph was taken before the addition of the color guard. In the background, from left to right, are Averi's Store, Nevy Brothers' Store, the doctor's office, and Louis Rose's store, which later became Joe Pluchinsky's Clover Farm Store, Sileck's Grocery, and then Joe Abramovich's Restaurant and Bar. (Courtesy of Albert Beres.)

UMWA Local 621 was in existence from 1933; its membership in 1948 was over 275. By 1973, the local was disbanded because membership was less than 10. (Courtesy of the Julius Morey collection.)

Union committee members are seen standing across the street from the company office in March 1940. From left to right are James Rubis, Steve Kish, and president of Local 621, John Biondo. (Courtesy of Inez Biondo Soorus and the Johnstown Tribune Democrat.)

To get his biweekly pay, the miner had to climb the stairs to the pay window on the landing, pick up his envelope, and exit via the other side of the stairs. Youngsters stood under the stairs, hoping to catch any loose coins that fell from the envelopes. On March 14, 1940, the miners exited the mines, expecting to be paid around $30,000. (Courtesy of Inez Biondo Soorus and the Johnstown Tribune Democrat.)

Union members pose on the stairs. Pictured from left to right are (first row) John Rubis, Charles "Fat Charlie" Hulchancy, Michael Totin and son Mickey, and Fred Michelbacher; (second row) ? Monyak, Jackson Molnar, Michael Balog, and Steve Kish; (third row) Albert "Katz" Oravec; (fourth row) John "Doby" Oravec, ? Leleck, and Joseph Babich; (fifth row) "Gentleman Jim" and James Rubis; (sixth row) Merle Hunter, Max Oravec, and Paul Pytash Sr.; (seventh row) John Biondo and Geno Simoncini. (Courtesy of Inez Biondo Soorus and the Johnstown Tribune Democrat.)

Town policeman and union member Charles Tourous was entrusted to keep order in town. He and other union members canvassed the town to see how many families were in desperate need of food. The company store was well stocked; the company refused to sell the food or trade it for back wages. Everything rotted and was taken away by a meat rendering company. Pictured at a union meeting are Louis Dusza in the first row, second from left, and Metro Rusinko at top right. (Courtesy of Inez Biondo Soorus and the Johnstown Tribune Democrat.)

The *Tribune Democrat* photographs capture the anxiety and fear in the faces of the miners. Some families did not qualify for relief because the fathers were not citizens. Shown in this photograph in the first row, from left to right are Alex "Big Alex" Oro, Joseph Kerekish, unidentified, and "Handlebar Pete." (Courtesy of Inez Biondo Soorus and the Johnstown Tribune Democrat.)

District two officials and lawyers arrived to advise the miners about all the legal repercussions of the offers from the company. Local 621 officers, from left to right, are (first row) Gabriel Toth, unidentified, John Biondo, Stephen Kish, and unidentified; (second row) Andrew Chekan, district two board member George Mottey, David Pesci, and James Rubis. (Courtesy of Inez Biondo Soorus and the Johnstown Tribune Democrat.)

The photographer assumed that these girls were the daughters of destitute miners. Two fathers were company men who were still on salary; another owned a barroom; and the last was a miner. From left to right are Aileen Cresswell, Jean Huth, Helen Farkas, and Catherine Hasen. (Courtesy of Inez Biondo Soorus and the Johnstown Tribune Democrat.)

The most poignant photograph of the series is that of the miners' wives. These women stand proud in the face of hardship. Immigrant wives worked as hard as their husbands. They cooked, cleaned, gardened, washed clothes by hand, raised the children, and kept boarders. These women were the backbone of the mining town. Seen here from left to right are Irene Barate (also spelled Bartina), Helen Medwick, and Julia Marcus (also spelled Markus). (Courtesy of Inez Biondo Soorus and the Johnstown Tribune Democrat.)

Local 621 leaders traveled to Washington, D.C., to speak to John L. Lewis, UMWA president. In turn, he contacted Frederic Delano who was able to help broker a settlement. Milton Brandon, president of Vinton Colliery Company, is signing an agreement. Seated at the table from left to right are John Biondo, Brandon, and unidentified. Witnessing the signing, from left to right, are Thomas Madigan, James Rubis, Allie Cresswell, Stephen Oblackovich, and Russell Dodson. (Courtesy of Inez Biondo Soorus and the Johnstown Tribune Democrat.)

Courts handled the reorganization, and the Vinton Coal and Coke Company emerged in 1943 in the first successful Chapter 11 bankruptcy in Pennsylvania. A $350,000 loan from Lewis Hicks of Pittsburgh was arranged to start up the company. The loan was paid back in 1945. In this photograph, unidentified miners and their wives are signing up for relief. (Courtesy of Inez Biondo Soorus and the Johnstown Tribune Democrat.)

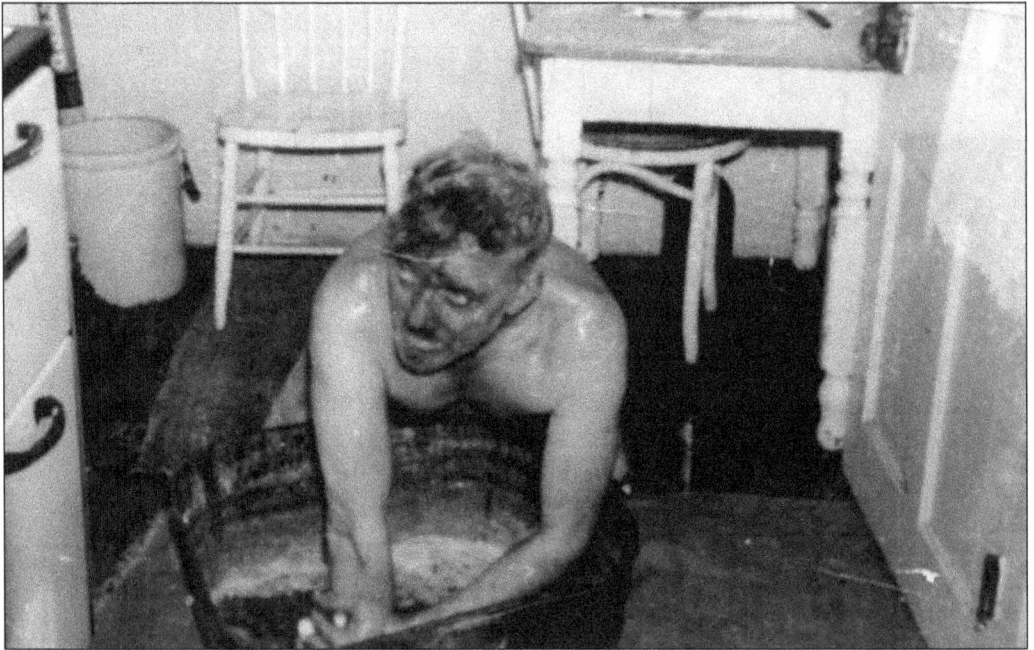

After a grueling day, the miners had to cross the flat and trudge up to a mile to get home. Awaiting them was a round washtub of steaming hot water and strong soap. In this photograph, George Swanson is taking his bath in the kitchen. Some miners had washing sheds in the backyards. (Courtesy of Harold Swanson.)

Harold Swanson is leaving for his next shift. The photograph was taken at the side entrance of the building that housed Sileck's Market. (Courtesy of Harold Swanson.)

Some union members owned trucks and hauled bony and delivered house coal. Julius Morey's trucks hauled the bony to the rock dump at No. 6. During the war, Morey painted a new truck with tar to protect it from corrosion. Louis Dusza worked at the No. 1 tipple and also hauled house coal. Here he is with his 1940 Chevrolet truck. (Courtesy of Diane Dusza.)

Andrew Beres, a ball player and trumpeter in the union band, studied to get his foreman's papers. He worked at No. 6 in the early 1940s. He is posing in his band uniform at the family home on Maple Street. His automobile is a 1937 Oldsmobile. (Courtesy of Albert Beres.)

After the company store fire, the office moved to the Vintondale Inn. The men stood in line waiting for the pay window to open. Payday in Vintondale in the early 1950s was caught on film by Harold Swanson. The wives also stood in line waiting to get the wages so they could go pay their bills at the local grocery stores. (Courtesy of Harold Swanson.)

Waiting for their pay envelopes are, from left to right, Joe "Egypt" Oravec, Bernie Shedlock, Mike Bugal, Paul Pytash, and unidentified. (Courtesy of Harold Swanson.)

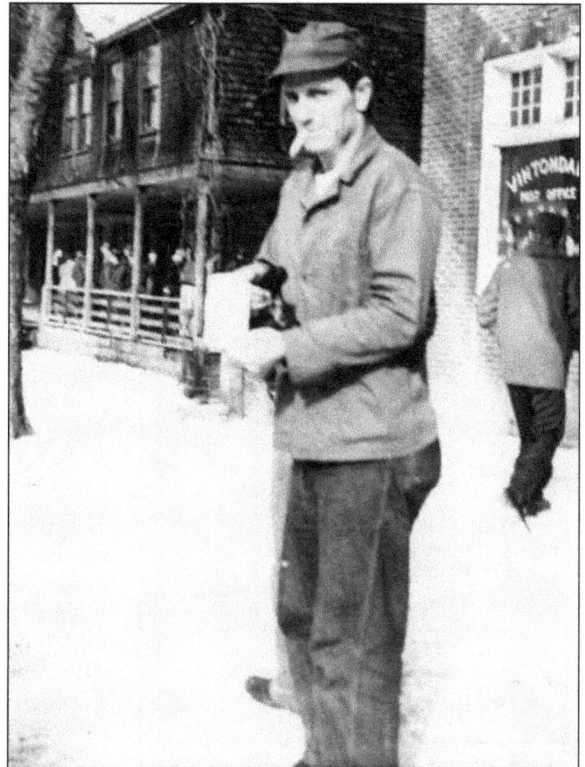

Paul Pytash is standing in front of the post office, which was formerly the Vintondale State Bank. The bank moved to Nanty Glo in 1937. (Courtesy of Harold Swanson.)

Another group of miners, including John Risko and Mark Reggetz are biding their time in front of Averi's Farmer Store. (Courtesy of Harold Swanson.)

This pay envelope belonged to Julius Morey and was issued by the reorganized Vinton Coal and Coke Company. Before unionization, many miners received "black snakes," which were black wavy lines indicating that there was no money in the pay. The miners owed more for rent, water, electricity, the doctor, and the company store than they had earned. Once John Morey's biweekly pay in 1938 was $2. (Courtesy of Julius Morey collection.)

Five

BUSINESSES

Between 1906 and 1930, there were up to 30 businesses in Vintondale. Several of the clothing stores were owned by Jewish merchants. Jacob and Sam Brett arrived when Vintondale's streets were nothing but a sea of mud. Their cousin Daniel Myers opened a butcher shop, and Freeman's had a clothing store in the Averi building. The only Jewish merchant who stayed for any length of time was Louis Rose, who had a clothing store at the corner of Third and Main Streets.

Hotels provided various types of accommodations for visitors and miners alike. The Vintondale Inn catered to salesmen and company men, while the Village Inn near the train station served lumbermen and railroaders. Other places to room were the Red Hotel and the Farkas Hotel. Liquor consumption had always been high, and there were two wholesale distributors before Prohibition, Farabaugh's and Callet's. Prohibition did not prevent the miners from obtaining alcohol. Many made their own and opened speakeasies. After Prohibition was repealed, Pushcar's (also spelled Puskar's), Joe Abromovich's, Nemesh's, Farkas Hotel, and the Hillside Club were open for business. The Veterans of Foreign Wars (VFW) and the Firemen's Club opened after World War II.

Grocery stores were located in all parts of town. Sam Williams opened his store on Third and Main Streets in 1902. On Plank Road, there were numerous Hungarian mom-and-pop stores, like Segedy's, Antal's, and Kerekish's. On the lower end, one found Bagu's, Mary Nancarvis', and Rosacha's. Nevy Brothers, who catered to the Italian populations in Vintondale, Wehrum, and Colver, opened their first store at the lower end of town. The store moved uptown when Gaal's Meat Market closed. Nevy Brothers store was sold to Charles Wilson in the late 1960s. In 1980, Jack and Joanne Vasilko purchased Wilson's Superette and operated the J and J Market until 2002.

Other early businesses included Walter "Butch" Morris's meat market, Sher's Jewelry, and Jacob's Garage. After the company store closed in 1940, Joseph Pluchinsky opened a Clover Farm store in the former Louis Rose store.

Gasoline became a necessary commodity as more residents purchased automobiles. The Vintondale Supply Company, Ltd. store; Iva Cook; Brett's; Nevy Brothers; Cresswell Electric; and Roberts' Esso all sold gasoline. Today a resident has to drive over five miles to pump gasoline. The only businesses in Vintondale today are an automobile repair shop, one bicycle shop, and an automobile salvage business.

VINTONDALE SUPPLY STORE, VINTONDALE, PA

The first company store of the Vinton Colliery Company was a wooden building located in Block A on Main Street. After the impressive new stone company store and office was finished in 1907, the old store, seen at the right, became a nickelodeon. (Courtesy of Betty and Theresa McDevitt.)

The store was well supplied with all the necessities of life, including groceries, meats, clothing, furniture, and mining supplies. Shown here from left to right, longtime employees in the 1930s were John Kuhar Sr.; Frances Wojtowicz Pluchinsky; Agnes Huth Dusza; unidentified; unidentified; and Joseph Pluchinsky, the butcher. The unidentified women may be Pearl Galardy and Katherine Makepeace. (Courtesy of Walter and Barbara Pluchinsky.)

56

Employees filled the orders that were charged to the miners' tabs. In hard times, the wives waited at the store for the daily tonnage rates to come from the mines to see how much they could purchase. Seen here are company teamsters who delivered items to the homes and to the mines. Steve Lantzy is second from the right, and company policeman Jack Butala is on the right. The pipes in the background provided hot water from the powerhouse for steam heat for the company buildings. The borough office and jail are in the rear. (Courtesy of George Lantzy.)

No   441   Vintondale, Pa.,   3-13-   19

DUE   Fred Michelbacher

ONE DOLLAR

in merchandise at the VINTON SUPPLY CO.

                                VINTON SUPPLY CO.

$1.00   Per

NOT GOOD IF DETACHED FROM BILL BELOW.   NOT TRANSFERABLE

Vintondale miners were often paid in paper scrip rather than in cash. The scrip could only be exchanged for goods at the company store, a win-win situation for the company. Mike Farkas sold beer and whiskey for scrip and then cashed in the scrip at the company store. When the company store closed on March 14, 1930, he was stuck with several hundred dollars of worthless scrip. (Courtesy of the Dusza family collection.)

In its heyday, the Vintondale Inn was a state-of-the-art hotel that catered to salesmen and company dignitaries. Many Vinton Colliery Company bosses and secretaries also boarded at the hotel. In the 1920s and 1930s, teachers boarded at the hotel. There was a funeral home in the basement in the early 1940s, and a short-lived Teen Canteen opened there in the 1950s. (Courtesy of Betty and Theresa McDevitt.)

The large four-bay hotel garage was located on the alley behind the hotel. Originally meant for caring for guests' horses and carriages, it housed guests' and hotel residents' automobiles. In the years between 1910 and 1920, very few people, except company personnel and the doctor, owned an automobile. The purchase of a new automobile became a news event in the local Nanty Glo paper. The haze in the background is from the coke ovens. (Courtesy of Betty and Theresa McDevitt.)

The Vintondale State Theater, another company subsidiary, opened in 1924 and replaced the nickelodeon that was in the old company store. Superintendent Otto Hoffman was fond of movies and encouraged the construction of the building. The last movies were shown around 1960, and the building was razed to build the new VFW. Martha Morey, holding her daughter Meri Clare, is standing in front of the theater marquis in 1946. (Courtesy of the Julius Morey collection.)

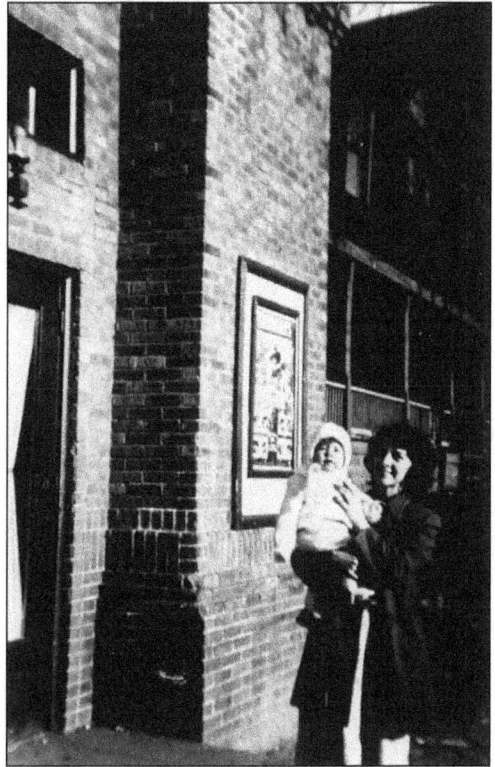

VINTONDALE STATE BANK
Vintondale, Pa.

Mr. John Morey, Sr.,

    Vintondale, Pa.

Dear Sir:--

    You have been allotted five shares of The Vintondale State Bank, Vintondale, Pa., at One Hundred and Ten Dollars per share, or a total of $ 550.00.

    One hundred dollars on each share will be applied to Capital Stock and Ten dollars per share to the Surplus Fund.

    Kindly forward your payments as follows to L. I. Arbogast, Treasurer, Vintondale, Pa.

    $35.00 per share on November 1st, 1923.

    $35.00 per share on December 1st, 1923.

    $40.00 per share on January 1st, 1924.

    You can make payment of the entire amount of your subscription on November 1st, if you desire.

    Thanking you for your interest in securing a Bank for Vintondale, we remain,

        Very truly yours,

                President.

In March 1923, Hoffman decided that $100,000 in postal savings stamps warranted opening a bank. Much of this money came from the sale of illegal liquor. Hoffman became the first president of the bank. After a town meeting to explain the idea, company officials canvassed the town to sell shares. As seen from the letter to John Morey Sr., the cost per share was $110. (Courtesy of the Julius Morey collection.)

Directors included Lloyd Arbogast, Mike Farkas, Samuel Freeman, George Balog, David Nevy, and I. E. Lewis. A brick bank building was erected beside the Vintondale Inn and opened on March 1, 1924. Teller Michael Mihalik kept the bank solvent during the Depression and it moved to Nanty Glo in 1937. In the 1950s, the post office moved into the building. Today it is the borough office. (Courtesy of Diane Dusza.)

Samuel Williams moved to Vintondale in 1902 to be closer to medical care; several children died of diphtheria on his farm near Strongstown. He operated a grocery store at Third and Main Streets. On one side of the second floor, Williams opened a Church of God. Williams also served as postmaster during the Republican administrations in the early 1900s. (Courtesy of Lloyd Williams.)

After Sam Williams's death, his daughter Sarah and her husband, Del George, took over the store, which became part of the Altoona-based Economy Stores franchise. Pictured in front of the store are the Georges' daughters, Ida and Ruth, along with Tom Kennedy. (Courtesy of Aileen Ure and Fred Michelbacher.)

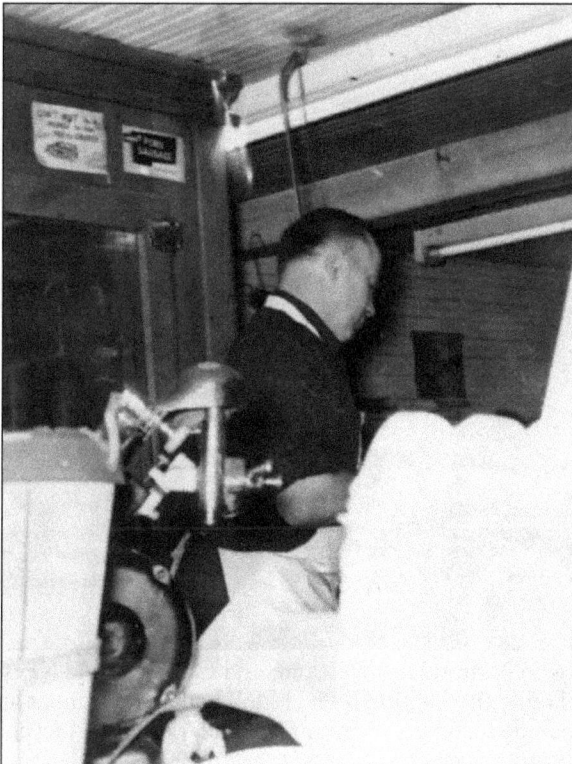

Del's poor health forced the Georges to retire in 1952. Lloyd Williams, Sarah's brother, took over the store. He had been injured in the mines and could not return to mining. In this photograph, Lloyd "Speedo" is cutting meat. In 1966, the store closed after Lloyd became the postmaster, like his father. (Courtesy of Harold Swanson.)

The five Nevy brothers, David, Charles, Ralph, Louie, and Henry, moved to Vintondale in 1915 and opened an Italian store at the lower end of town. They moved uptown to the Averi building and then to Gaal's, where they erected a two-story building. David saw a ready market for pasta and found the right location in Cumberland. Here the Nevy brothers opened the Cumberland Macaroni Factory. (Courtesy of Julius Morey.)

The Nevy Brothers store catered to Italians in Vintondale, Wehrum, and Colver. Louie Nevy and wife Italina lived above the store, and Frank and Pauline (Nevy) Pioli had an apartment at the rear of the store. The occasion for the parade seen here is unknown. Seen riding the bicycle on the left is David Dusza. (Courtesy of Edward Hagens.)

Alpine Eagle, the Nevy brothers' signature pasta, was packaged in bright blue boxes. During the Depression, sales were very good, and Alpine Eagle brand was even served at the White House. All of the Nevys left for Cumberland except Louie, who was the Italian store's butcher. His brother-in-law Joe Pioli was a longtime store employee. Louie's son Eddie sold the factory in 1994, and it permanently closed in 2000. (Courtesy of Denise Weber.)

Raymond "Biff" Cresswell and his wife, Lena, were the proprietors of the Cresswell Electric Company, which sold all kinds of electrical supplies, tires, automobile supplies, appliances, and gasoline. After Lena retired, the building was remodeled into apartments. (Courtesy of the Julius Morey collection.)

GUSES AUTO SERVICE
AUTOMOTIVE ENGINEERS
FOOT OF 3RD STREET

VINTONDALE, PA.

J. Morey
1-5-56

Remove Rear Wheels - check wheel cyl C
Clean - loosen brake shoes
adj - bleed   12.50

Replace Brake line   3.50
Repair - Replace carburetor   3.50

Replace Cyl Head (with help)   26.00
Replace old with new ring pinch   2.50
                                              $48.00

Paid Jan 13 - 1956

Guses Auto Service was owned by Gus Rogalski, who advertised himself as an automotive engineer. His first garage was a single-bay, wooden building at the foot of Third Street. A three-bay, cement block garage replaced the old one. The business became a full time operation after the mines closed. (Courtesy of the Julius Morey collection.)

Mike Farkas bought the grocery store and barroom in 1908 for $4,300. He ran the grocery store and leased the barroom to Joseph Shoemaker. After a miner tampering with blasting caps blew out part of a wall, Farkas added the mansard roof to make more room for boarders. Farkas, through various means, some of which were questionable, had built up a sizeable estate. He died in 1943 after falling down the cellar stairs. (Courtesy of George Lantzy.)

64

Farkas and his second wife, Helen Horvath Dusza-Farkas-Firko, ran the hotel. Farkas was bilingual, and the company utilized him to recruit miners. His moving truck was in use because of evictions and job switching. Appointing him to the bank board was a necessity. Not only could he influence miners to use the bank, but he himself had money to invest. Hungarian families were in his debt for the pigs he sold to them in the spring. The families raised the pigs and then butchered them in the fall. (Courtesy of George Lantzy.)

After Farkas's death, the hotel was run mainly by Helen's son, Steve Dusza. It was razed in 1974. (Courtesy of Diane Dusza.)

Roberts Service Center was opened in the late 1940s by Roy Roberts, a plumber for the Clinton Coal and Coke Company. Roy's sons, Richard and William, ran the station in the 1950s. (Courtesy of Harold Swanson.)

William Roberts is seen here pumping gas. (Courtesy of Harold Swanson.)

In the 1950s, Roberts' Esso station was the hangout for the high school boys. Here David Dusza is walking to the station to work. While in the air force, Dusza arranged his leave time so that he could run the station while the Roberts family went on vacation. In the background are the No. 1 mine rock dumps. The mine closed in 1948. (Courtesy of Harold Swanson.)

Richard Roberts is adding a quart of oil to this truck. (Courtesy of Harold Swanson.)

Loafing inside the station, from left to right, are Thomas Wray, David Dusza, Lewis Ure, and Manny Verba. (Courtesy of Harold Swanson.)

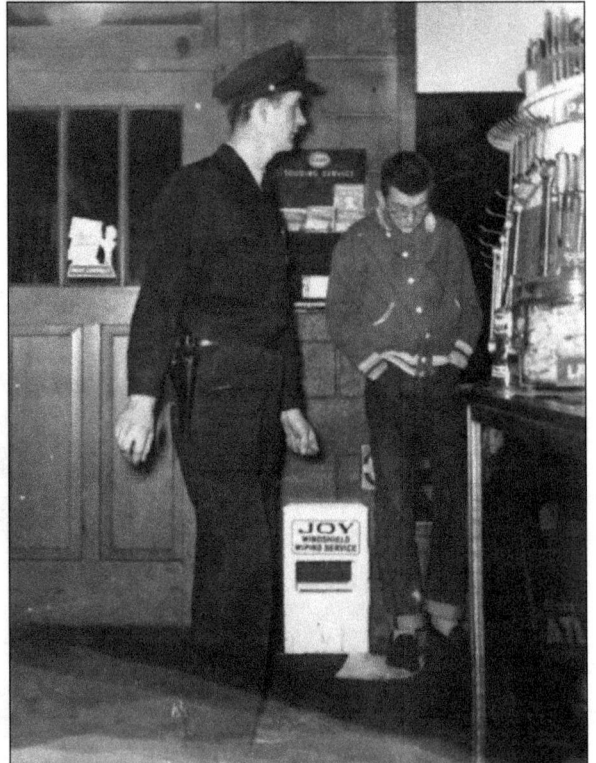

Even the town's policeman, Bruce Butala, stopped in when making his rounds about town. Wray is standing in the background. (Courtesy of Harold Swanson.)

Steve "Dilly" Pytash (right) and an unidentified person discuss events of the day. After Roy Robert's untimely, accidental death, William Roberts operated the garage. Several additional bays were added to the garage. These were destroyed in the 1977 flood. William Roberts Jr. and his brother Douglas operated the station as a repair shop until around 2004. (Courtesy of Harold Swanson.)

In 1913, Vintondale incorporated its volunteer fire company. Its volunteers have battled every type of fire, especially flue and grass fires. The junior firemen were dismissed from school to help fight the fires. In 1937, the department purchased a new pumper. Seen in the photograph from left to right are Carl and Frederick Michelbacher, unidentified, and Louis Dusza. (Courtesy of Aileen Ure and Fred Michelbacher.)

Before 1944, a hospital trip was called "dump truck service" because there was no ambulance and the roads were retched. Injured miners were transported by dump truck. A used Reo ambulance was bought in 1944, and in 1948, the fire company purchased a new custom built, grey, Cadillac ambulance for $7,500. The annual ambulance dues were $5, which did not meet the operating costs of the service. Fire company ambulance service stopped in 1966. (Courtesy of Edward Hagens.)

The fire company purchased a liquor license in 1948 and rented a barroom in the old Puskar (also spelled Pushcar) building from Steve Kish. In 1957, they purchased the building outright and built a garage in the basement to house the fire trucks and equipment. The Fire Ladies' Auxiliary, organized in 1940, raised money for the company. In the photograph are the future VFW on the left and the future Firemen's Club on the right. John Panes is standing facing Main Street. Leona Clasrson Dusza is leaving the post office. The boy is unidentified. (Courtesy of Albert Beres.)

The H. B. Daly Post 7211 of the VFW, organized in 1946, purchased the former Walter Morris butcher shop and converted it into a barroom. The Fire Ladies' Auxiliary and the War Mothers held meetings and grocery bingos in the upstairs rooms. In 1964, the post sold their old building and built a new one on the sites of the Vintondale Inn and the Vintondale State Theater. The old building was remodeled into apartments. (Courtesy of Diane Dusza.)

On May 30, 2005, the 60th anniversary of the end of World War II, the post dedicated an honor roll of Vintondale residents, male and female, who served in the war. Due to the tireless efforts of Joseph Gresko and Charles Sago, the names of 340 veterans were recognized. Fifteen of them died in the war, including Herbert Daly, John Bristsky, Frank Hegedus, Ernest Kerekes, John Kozar, Michael Kozar, George Larish, George Lybarger, David Mack, Michael Nemetz, John Regetz, Anthony Scenna, George Slippy, Joseph Wojtowicz, and William Wright. The bells at Ss. Peter and Paul Russian Orthodox Church tolled each time the name of a fatality was read. (Courtesy of Diane Dusza.)

Synopsis of Scenes

The entire action of the play takes place in the living room of the Woodruff family in a medium-sized Eastern town.

TIME: The present.

ACT I. Late afternoon in June.

ACT II. Afternoon; two weeks later.

ACT III. Noon; two weeks later.

The class of 1941 presented their senior class play at the Vintondale State Theater. The advertisements are important to show the variety of businesses that were located in Vintondale.

CAST OF CHARACTERS

Mrs. Chester Woodruff, who loves to go to
    funerals _____ HELEN FARKAS
Chester Woodruff, her husband, who loves
    to go to fires _____ JOHN GREGOR
Junior Woodruff, their son, who loves
    explosions _____ NICK HOZIK
Boots Woodruff, their daughter, who loves
    to act _____ HELEN KOVACH
Arlene Woodruff, their adopted daughter,
    who loves them all _____ JEAN HUTH
Zenith, the Woodruff maid, who loves to
    escape work _____ ANNE GABODA
Aunt Cora, who loves to complain _ EMMA JANE DALY
Mrs. Margaret Taylor, who loves to
    visit _____ CATHERINE HASEN
Bunny Taylor, her daughter, who loves to
    have her own way _____ AILEEN CRESWELL
Homer Hampton Haywood, who loves to
    promote _____ EUGENE GIAZZON
Wade Wainright, who loves Arlene ____ JAMES TOTIN
Chetwynde Cluett, who loves making folks
    happy _____ JOHN HALUPKA

5

(Courtesy of Jean Huth Hammer.)

In 1974, many of the abandoned buildings in downtown were eyesores and were razed. The former Sileck's Grocery and Joe Abromovich's bar were torn down, and in 1981, the site became the new Firemen's Club. The firemen's old building was torched in the "Friend of a Friend" terror threat. (Courtesy of Diane Dusza.)

There are only five of the original commercial buildings remaining on upper Main Street, including the Farabaugh building (Cresswell's), Walter Morris' Meat Market (old VFW), Nevy's (J and J Market), Freeman's (Averi's and Colangelo's), and Williams' Economy Store. None host any commercial activity. (Courtesy of Diane Dusza.)

Six

DISASTERS

Vintondale seems to be sheltered from all outside influences in its seemingly serene valley, but Mother Nature called occasionally with a vengeance. The borough has been subjected to numerous floods, but none as devastating as the 1977 Johnstown Flood. Damages were estimated at over $1 million.

Not as widespread, but as equally terrifying, have been two tornadoes that struck in 1919 and in 1998. In 1919, many of the buildings at No. 6 were heavily damaged. In 1998, most of the damage was limited to fallen tree limbs, except at Lloyd Williams's house. The large, 100-year-old beech tree in his backyard was uprooted by high winds and fell directly onto his house.

Fires are always a plague in a mining town, and Vintondale has had its share of serious fires. In 1943, the company store and office building burned to the ground, and in 1945 the coal washery went up in flames within minutes. The progress of the fire was caught on film. That fire was the death knell of coke operations in Vintondale.

In 1980 and 1981, Vintondale was terrorized by one or more individuals who have yet to be identified. The terror threats started on May 18, 1980, with the bombing of the People's Savings and Loan in Nanty Glo. On June 4, 1980, an explosion caused $10,000 damage to St. Charles Church in Twin Rocks. A bomb, which did not go off, was found at Mayor Stephen Oblackovich's home the same day. In October 1980, raw asbestos and a petroleum substance were dumped into the Shuman Run reservoir leaving 800 people without water service. Threatening letters were also sent to various members of the community. Several fires, mainly targeting the barrooms, were set. The Citizen's Club on Chickaree Hill went up in flames. The new VFW was torched in December 1979, but the building was so airtight that the fire burned itself out. The Firemen's Club burned on March 9, 1980. The last fire was tragic beyond belief. On December 8, 1980, fire was set to the Nemesh Hotel, and Charlie Nemesh and his wife, Anna, burned to death. The target of the terror campaign was Stephen Oblackovich, Vintondale's mayor and county clerk of courts. A grand jury convened in Pittsburgh to hear testimony on the bombings and mail threats. No arrests were made as a result of the grand jury hearing, and the testimony was sealed.

The Vinton Colliery Company store and office building caught fire about 11:00 p.m. on January 16, 1943. The store closed in the 1940 bankruptcy, but the company maintained its offices upstairs. The ground floor became a community center. Aileen Huth Michelbacher-Ure rushed upstairs to save the timecards. She said, "I was ok; the fire was in attic; and I wanted to save all the records." The firemen kept calling her to come down before it was too late. Ure, age 92, obviously heeded that advice and safely exited the building. (Courtesy of Huth family collection.)

January 17, 1943, was a scheduled payday, but the miners threatened a walkout. That threat saved the payroll from being destroyed in the fire. The fire knocked out telephone exchange right away, and the firemen could not call out for help. The Nanty Glo Fire Company had to be summoned by automobile. The fire was out of control when the Nanty Glo firemen arrived, so they concentrated on saving nearby buildings. (Courtesy of Charles Sago.)

The first and second floors collapsed into the basement. The estimated loss was $15,000, and the cause was ruled electrical. The coal company moved its offices to the first floor of the Vintondale Inn, known to those who grew up in the 1950s as the Union Hall. (Courtesy of Charles Sago.)

Much of the stone from the store was used for building walls around Vintondale, especially on Griffith Street. Roberto Ugoletti from Dilltown was the stone mason. Here a bulldozer can be seen moving the debris from the basement of the store. (Courtesy of Julius Morey collection.)

The walls and gaping hole that had been the company store was a hazard for over 25 years. It was finally demolished and a community park with a fountain was built on the site. (Courtesy of Diane Dusza.)

The park disappeared when the U.S. Postal Service decided to build a new post office rather than pay a higher rent for use of the old bank building. (Courtesy of Diane Dusza.)

The most spectacular fire was at the coal washery, which was photographed as the fire quickly consumed the brick building. Built in 1906, its purpose was to wash impurities out of the coking coal. On February 16, 1945, a fire broke out before noon in the area of the heating plant. Within 20 minutes, the whole structure was engulfed in flames because of the coal dust and high winds. (Courtesy of Beulah Ling Bracken.)

The Nanty Glo firemen concentrated on keeping the fire from spreading to the tipple while Vintondale firemen labored to control the washery fire. At 4:30 p.m., a second fire broke out in the roof of the powerhouse. Water to fight the fire came from the Blacklick Creek and from a railroad water tank above the black bridge. Two Pennsylvania Railroad steam engines shuttled back and forth from the standpipe. (Courtesy of Beulah Ling Bracken.)

Six Vintondale firemen suffered burns on their hands and faces and were treated by Dr. Michael Long, including fire chief Alfred Pioli, Steve Oblackovich, James Balog, Joseph Vascovich, Michael Brozina, and Julius Morey. (Courtesy of Beulah Ling Bracken.)

Loss to the washery building was between $30,000 and $50,000, but the long-term loss to Vintondale was immeasurable. With the loss of the washery, coke production ceased after 39 years. (Courtesy of Beulah Ling Bracken.)

Beulah Ling Bracken was standing on the bank behind Nevy Brothers store and photographed the dramatic scenes. Other pictures were taken by Thomas Kasper, and the film was not developed until 1998. (Courtesy of Joanne Kasper Vasilko.)

Following the demise of No. 6 in 1968, there were few major fires until the outbreak of mysterious fires aimed at the barrooms in town. Torched were the Fireman's Club (formerly Pushcar's), the new VFW, the Citizens' Club (Hillside Club) on Chickaree Hill, and the Nemesh Hotel. This "Friend of a Friend" terrorist campaign resulted in the murders of Charles and Anna Nemesh, who died in the arson fire at their hotel on December 10, 1980. (Courtesy of Diane Dusza.)

Although most people do not think of Pennsylvania as tornado prone, several tornados have hit Vintondale. In 1919 or 1920, a powerful storm whipped through the valley. It blew the steeple off the Baptist church and moved on to the No. 6 flat. Part of the roof of the washery blew away and part of the west wall collapsed. The roof of the powerhouse collapsed onto the machinery. (Courtesy of Betty and Theresa McDevitt.)

On June 30, 1998, an F-0 tornado or "gustnado" started in Vintondale and ricocheted up the valley, bouncing from one hill to another as far away as Nanty Glo. The storm, part of a widespread severe weather front that moved in from Ohio, took out trees as it moved up the Blacklick Valley. The largest downed tree was at Lloyd Williams's house on Third Street. (Courtesy of Fr. Donald Dusza.)

A 100-year-old beech tree in the Williams family's backyard was uprooted and landed squarely on the Williams' house, yet the only damage next door was a gas grill that was tossed into the front yard. Lloyd Williams and his daughter Sandy were not home at the time. (Courtesy of Denise Weber.)

The lower end of Vintondale is on a flood plain. In the March 1936 flood, the Blacklick Creek overflowed and flooded the first floors of the houses near the Hungarian Church. The most devastating flood arrived on July 19 and 20, 1977. Thunderstorms stalled over the Johnstown and dumped over 11 inches of rain in 10 hours. The thunder and lightning lasted all night. Rising flood waters forced residents to take emergency measures. (Courtesy of Walter and Barbara Pluchinsky.)

Water gushed down the hills, washing out roads and bridges and sweeping away cars under its crushing power. As the Blacklick Creek started rising, families at the lower end of town began to move furniture to their second floors. In the meantime, debris carried by the flood began to jam up behind the cement bridge by the railroad. (Courtesy of Julius Morey collection.)

Around 3:00 a.m., the flood waters cut across the tennis courts and smashed into the Zakraycek's and the Kerekes' houses, knocking them off of their foundations. The Crawfords' house, located next door, stopped them from washing downstream. Ten people were trapped in the Kerekes' house and in dire danger of drowning. Donny Kerekes, his mother Irene, his grandmother and his nephew had been joined earlier in the night by Clair Crawford and his family. The Crawfords' house did not have a basement, and they went to the Kerekes' house when the water began rising. (Courtesy of Nanty Glo Journal.)

Rescue attempts by boat failed due to the swift current. At daybreak, volunteers formed a ladder brigade to reach the trapped people. The rescuers had to scale the side of Zakraysek's house, cross its roof and pull the people out of the side window of Kerekes' house. Survivors, including Irene Kerekes' 80-year-old mother, were lifted out of the house and carried on ladders over the roof and down the side of the Zakraysek's house. (Courtesy of Julius Morey collection.)

Shuman Run raged out of control and washed out a large part of Roberts' Exxon station. (Courtesy of Julius Morey collection.)

Debris in Shuman Run blocked the drain under Plank Road, and the flood water washed out the road, cutting Vintondale in two. (Courtesy of the Julius Morey collection.)

Heavy equipment had to be brought in to help fill in the gap in Plank Road. Shuman Run tore up the pavement on First Street (Dinkey Street) and took out 20 to 30 feet of the yards on the Plank Road side of the creek. (Courtesy of the Julius Morey collection.)

After the waters receded, the backbreaking clean up of mud, debris, trees, cars, and appliances had to be done. The Crawford's house (left) survived the flood and probably kept the overturned houses from washing away. Joseph Beltz's house is on the right. (Courtesy of the Nanty Glo Journal.)

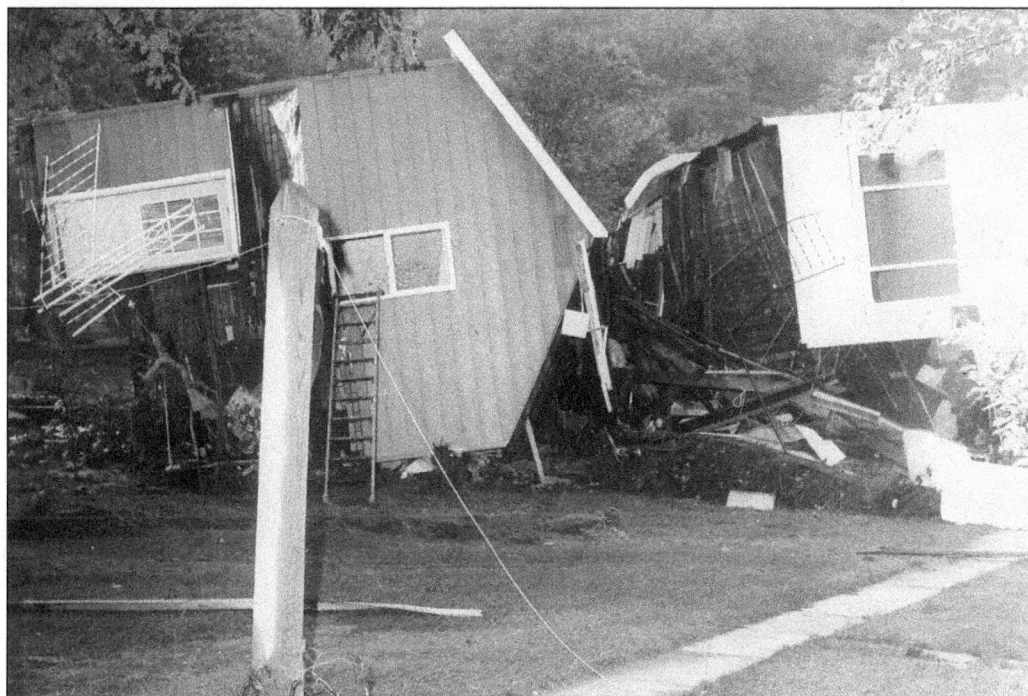

The Kerekish house, where 10 people had to be rescued, is on the right. The Zakraysek house is on the left. (Courtesy of the Nanty Glo Journal.)

Harold Swanson lived in the last house on Main Street. His living quarters were on the second floor of the house. As the water rose, he and his wife, Arlene, devised a plan to get out of the house with their two children, using an upturned table as a raft. The water reached the top of the stairs and then began to recede. (Courtesy of Harold Swanson.)

This garage floated down into Tony Gerley's yard. (Courtesy of the Nanty Glo Journal.)

Joseph Beltz is shoveling away mud that his son Dennis has just heaved out the cellar window. Dennis's trailer in the backyard was washed away. Later Dennis and his family moved into the family house, and Joseph and his wife, Mary, moved into a new trailer in the backyard. (Courtesy of the Nanty Glo Journal.)

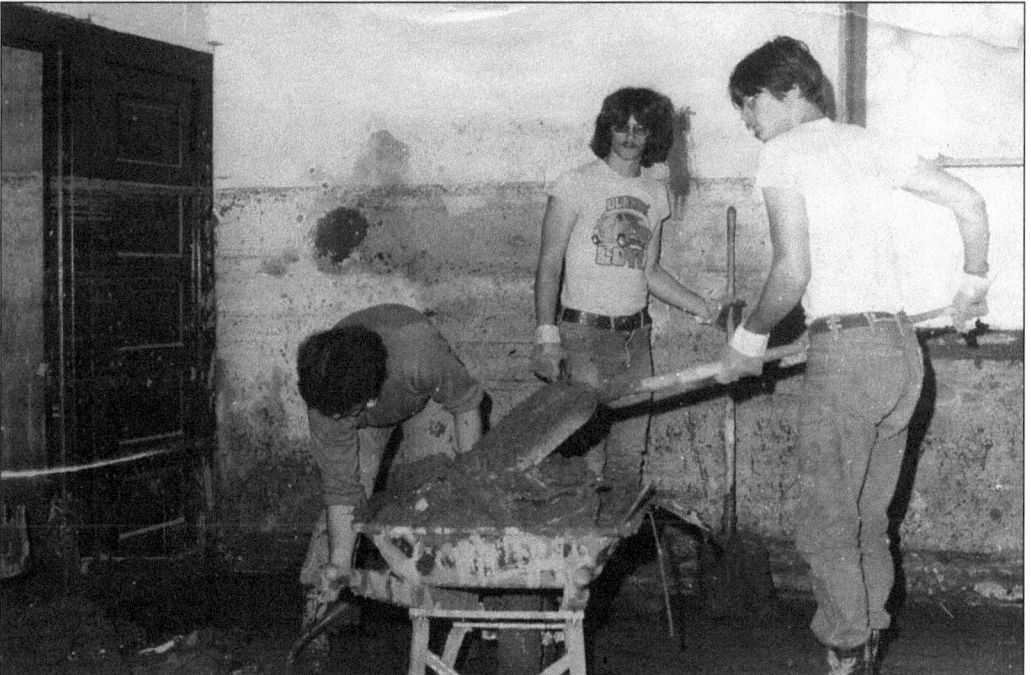

Clean up began as soon as the water receded. Shoveling out the basement of the Hungarian Church, from left to right, are Gregory Kovach, Douglas Kuhar, and ? Kuhar. (Courtesy of the Nanty Glo Journal.)

The Firemen's Club became the relief center. Donations of food and clothing poured into Vintondale. Feeding volunteers was another task of the relief center. Mary Ann Donaldson Smith (foreground) and Mary Mayancsik (center) are assisting in serving meals. Others in the photograph are unidentified. (Courtesy of the Nanty Glo Journal.)

Donations of clothing were sorted and made available at the Firemen's Club. Names of those in the photograph are unknown. (Courtesy of the Nanty Glo Journal.)

Seven

CHURCHES AND SCHOOLS

Religion has always played a major role in the lives of Vintondale's residents. As early as 1895, a Baptist church was organized, followed by Samuel Williams' Church of God. The Roman Catholic church was built in 1902. In 1907, Ss. Peter and Paul Russian Orthodox Church moved to Vintondale from Wehrum. The Hungarian Reformed Church was organized in 1914. The Jehovah's Witnesses splintered off from the Orthodox Church and purchased a building for a Kingdom Hall in the 1950s.

In spite of Vintondale's reputation as a "wild and woolly" mining camp, education was important. The Vinton Colliery Company took a controlling interest in the schools. The superintendent's wife served as the president of the school board. To consolidate its classrooms, the district built a six room, brick building at the top of Fourth Street in 1913, followed by a second brick building next to it. The second building burned in 1930 and was replaced by the Delano building. Vintondale opened the first three-year high school in the Blacklick Valley in 1916 and accepted students from Wehrum, Twin Rocks, and Nanty Glo. In 1927, Vintondale constructed the first four-year high school in the community park at Second and Griffith Streets. Charles Mower served as the supervising principal from 1923 to 1970.

The Depression hit the school district hard. The company was behind on its property taxes. School supplies and textbooks were scarce. Needed repairs, like painting and fixing the heating system, were not addressed. Tax problems were not solved until 1943 when the company emerged from bankruptcy.

During World War II, class sizes were affected by early enlistments. Mower, a World War I veteran, re-enlisted in the service. Faculty members were not exempt from the draft board, making it difficult to find substitutes.

In 1955, Vintondale schools joined with Nanty Glo to form the Nanty Glo–Vintondale Joint School District. The new jointure planned to build a new high school, which was not constructed until Blacklick Township District joined Blacklick Valley School District. After consolidation, Vintondale students had weekly art and music lessons. Football was available to the Vintondale boys, but the separate basketball teams ended. Between 1957 and 1960, both high schools remained opened. In the fall of 1960, Vintondale High School closed and was converted to an elementary school. The high school students were bussed to Nanty Glo.

The First Baptist Church was founded in 1895, and the church was dedicated on October 3, 1897. For many years, the church was affiliated with the Baptist Church in Dilltown. Rev. Edward Houser was the pastor. Today the church has a resident pastor. (Courtesy of Diane Dusza.)

Hungarian Reformed Church catered to the Hungarians of Protestant leanings. The Hungarians who were Catholic attended the Catholic Church or the Byzantine Church in Nanty Glo. The present church was built in 1930 following a fire. At one time, there was a resident pastor, but today the number of parishioners has dwindled to less than 10. Services are held once a month by a minister from Johnstown or from the Bethlen Home in Ligonier. (Courtesy of Diane Dusza.)

The Kingdom Hall opened in the mid-1950s. Most of its members had splintered from the Russian Orthodox Church in the early 1920s. The Vintondale Kingdom Hall disbanded in 1973 and joined up with the one in Mundays Corner. (Courtesy of Harold Swanson.)

Ss. Peter and Paul Russian Orthodox Church had its origins in Wehrum. When Wehrum suffered a shutdown for about two years, the congregation moved to Vintondale and built at church at the top of Third Street on a lot purchased from Judge Augustine Vinton Barker. Until the 1950s, the parish had a resident priest. Today the priest serves parishes in Portage and in Vintondale and maintains his residence in Portage. (Courtesy of Diane Dusza.)

Ss. Peter and Paul Russian Orthodox Church celebrated its 100th anniversary with a special Divine Liturgy on Sunday, September 2, 2007. In attendance were many descendents of the original members. To mark the occasion, the church underwent a major restoration. New window frames and wainscoting were installed, the brass chandeliers were refurbished, and a wooden ceiling was installed. In this 1992 photograph, Ann Balog is giving a guided tour to visitors at the Rails to Trails celebration. (Courtesy of Denise Weber.)

Immaculate Conception Roman Catholic Church, now Ss. Timothy and Mark Chapel, was built in 1902 on Fourth Street on lots donated by the Vinton Colliery Company. Various remodeling projects over the years have totally changed the interior and exterior of the church. The neo-Gothic altars were removed in the 1950s, and the church was encased in yellow brick in the 1960s. Fr. John Callan's inside renovations of the 1950s have since disappeared. The parish is proud to have two native sons who have joined the priesthood. Fr. Donald Dusza is a priest with the Altoona-Johnstown Diocese, and Fr. Wesley Mash is a priest in the Byzantine Rite. (Courtesy of Diane Dusza.)

94

Seen in this photograph is the First Communion class of 1937. The pastor is Fr. Charles Gallagher, and the catechism teachers are Sarah McQuaide (second row, left) and Mary Grosik (fourth row, left). The altar boy on the left is Bernard "Binkey" McConnell, and the flower girl in the first row on the right is Carol Huth. Among the first communicants is Catherine "Bootsy" Rafas, in the second row, second from left. (Courtesy of the Huth family collection.)

In the 1950s and 1960s, the Sisters of Charity from Johnstown taught catechism on Saturday mornings. From left to right are (first row) Paulette Kangur, Meri Clare Morey, and Arlene Drabbant; (second row) Carolyn Tackett, Ivanna Dotts, and Diane Dusza; (third row) Helen "Tootsie" Shamko, unidentified, Sister Mary Clement, S.C., and Bernadette Wojtowicz. (Courtesy of Denise Weber.)

This six-room, brick building was erected in 1913. The old building was abandoned when the high school students began traveling to Nanty Glo for classes. It was demolished in 1985. (Courtesy of Betty and Theresa McDevitt.)

The Delano School building was built in 1930 to replace the school that burned to the ground. It served fifth through eighth grades and was demolished in 1985. (Courtesy of Diane Dusza.)

Vintondale offered the first three-year high school in the Blacklick Valley and the first four-year high school, seen here. It was built in 1926 and 1927. After all Vintondale students were bussed to Nanty Glo, the building became a senior citizens' center and was also used for catechism or Confraternity of Christian Doctrine (CCD) classes by the Catholic churches in Vintondale and Twin Rocks. (Courtesy of Diane Dusza.)

Charles Mower served as principal of Vintondale Public Schools between 1927 and 1970, save for a stint in the service during World War II. In the summers, he and Zoltan Antol motorcycled across the country to Arizona to take graduate courses. This photograph was taken on one of Mower's cross-country trips or on one of his many fishing trips to Canada. (Courtesy of the Vintondale Homecoming Committee.)

Vintondale High School occasionally held proms in the auditorium of the school. In 1951, the chaperones were photographed for the dance. Pictured from left to right are (first row) Mrs. Charles Turous, Katherine Lybarger, Catherine Wray, Ruth Horne, Agnes Dusza, Claire Sebulsky, Hazel Oblackovich, and Ann Pioli; (second row) Max Oravec, Charles Mower, Charles Turous, Zoltan Antol, Oscar "Pete" Wray, George Sileck, Steve Dusza, Richard Sebulsky, Stephen Oblackovich, and Alfred Pioli. (Courtesy of the Vintondale Homecoming Committee.)

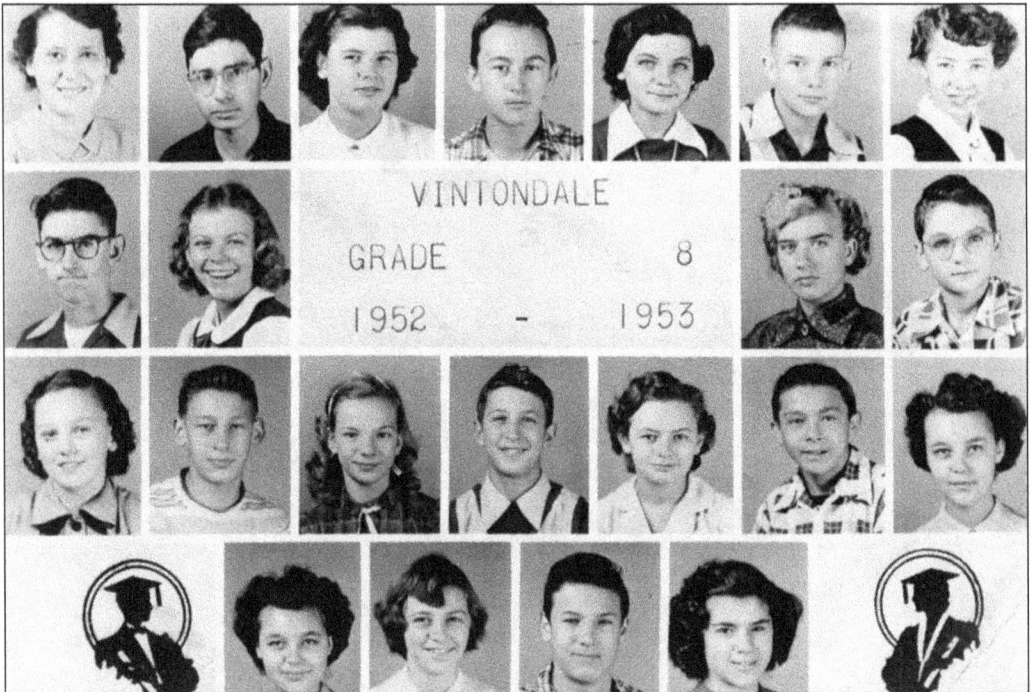

Catherine Wray taught the 1952–1953 eighth-grade class. Seen here from left to right are (first row) Wray, Robert "Bobbie" Frantz, Dorothy Sheesley, John Gresko, Barbara Karol, Thomas Wray, and Judy Morey; (second row) James Sheesley, Catherine "Sis" Lybarger, Elaine Marcus, and Robert Karol; (third row) Maryetta Misner, Thomas Hegedus, Edith Ambrose, David Dusza, Dorothy Garvis, Paul Luzar, and Anna Nemish; (fourth row) Mary Nemish, Catherine "Kushy" Bugal, George Telesko, and Dorothy Shestak. (Courtesy of the Dusza family collection.)

The 1956–1957 junior-class officers included, from left to right, (first row) Anita Selip, Anna May Branick, and Joanne Casper; (second row) advisor Peter Previte and Michael Gresko. (Courtesy of the Vintondale Homecoming Committee.)

The 1956–1957 freshman-class officers included, from left to right, (first row) Betty Oravec, advisor Zoltan Antol, and Marge Glowa; (second row) Gus Oravec, and John "Sonny" Kuhar. (Courtesy of the Vintondale Homecoming Committee.)

The 1956–1957 Rod and Gun Club officers , from left to right, were (first row) Stephen John Kish, advisor Zoltan Antol, and Paul Luzar; (second row) George Berish and Michael "Red" Gresko. (Courtesy of the Vintondale Homecoming Committee.)

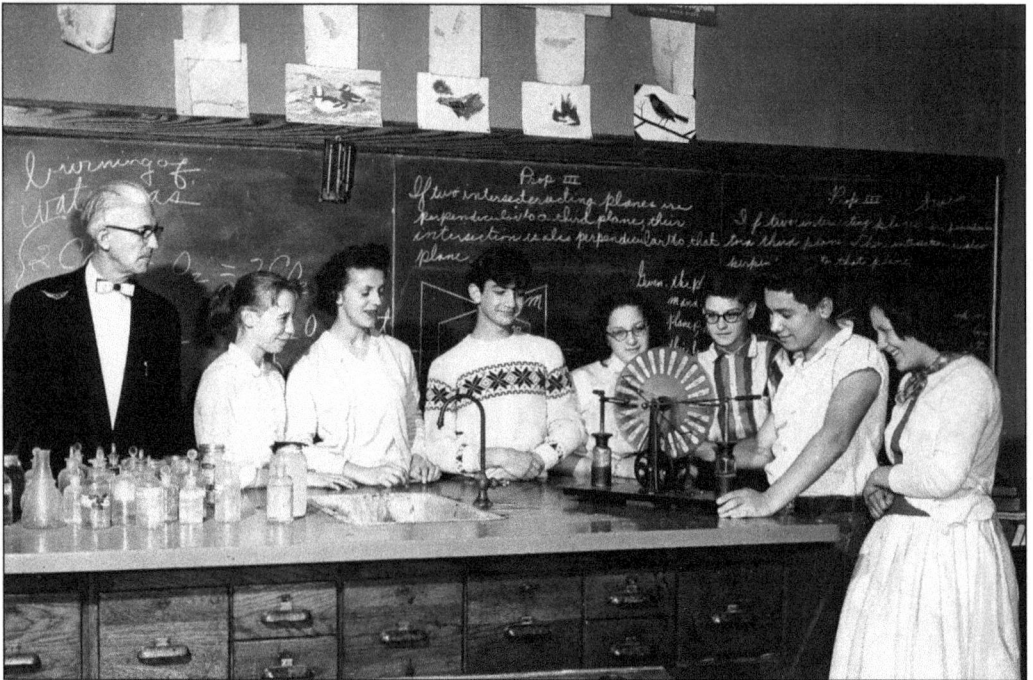

The Science Club's advisor was Charles Mower, seen at left. Members seen here, from left to right, are Barbara Mazey, Margaret Glowa, Edward Pytash, Dorothy Jacobs, John Frantz, Donald Kerekes, and Betty Telesko. (Courtesy of the Vintondale Homecoming Committee.)

In this photograph from the 1957 Nanty Glo–Vintondale yearbook, Vintondale Varsity Club is pictured on the Nanty Glo football field. From left to right are George Pytash, Michael Shamko, George Berish, Michael Gresko, John McPherson, William Wray, Gerald Beltz, Thomas Hodge, Stephen Kish, David Dusza, Paul Krousick, David Kerekes, Donald Kolar, advisor Peter Previte, Roger "Jamie" James, John Grosik, Gerald Donaldson, Donald Kerekes, John Frantz, Dominick Averi, John Kuhar, Robert Drabbant, Paul Luzar, William Wray, Joseph Silep, and Joseph Mesoras. (Courtesy of the Vintondale Homecoming Committee.)

Returning to Vintondale for the annual homecoming were two former teachers who both lived to be over 100 years old. Helen Brozina (second from the right) taught second grade, and her sister, May Crouse, taught fifth grade in the Vintondale schools. Brozina retired to Florida where she died in 2007. Seen with her in this 1981 photograph, from left to right, are Julia Holupka Pytash, Ellen Pioli Pisarcik, and Mary Yanko Bianucci. (Courtesy of Jean Huth Hammer.)

Mary Burr Carbaugh (seated second from right), who also lived to be 100, visited at the homecoming in 1994. She taught seventh and eighth grades. She died in 2004. Pictured at left is Joanne Kasper Vasilko and to the right is Burr Carbaugh's son Stephens Burr. (Courtesy of Denise Weber.)

The high school boys decided to construct a snowman in the high school yard in 1958 or 1959. Dennis Dusza, age three, is standing beside the snowman. (Courtesy of Diane Dusza.)

Eight

SPORTS AND RECREATION

In Vintondale, the Vinton Colliery Company strongly influenced sports. The company sponsored baseball teams in 1906 or even earlier. Most baseball players had outside jobs and often were able to leave work early on game day. Basketball also received a lot of company and community support in the 1920s and 1930s. Most of that support went to the girls' teams. By 1934, the girls had gone 34 games without a loss. The company supported the basketball teams by providing court space in the social hall.

High school sports ceased when Michael Hozik was drafted during World War II. They were not revived until 1946. Alfred Pioli became the basketball coach, but there was nowhere to practice. The town social hall had been torn down. Arrangements were made with the Blacklick School District to use its basketball court. The Vintondale basketball team began its losing streak that lasted until 1955.

The baseball teams also lost members to enlistments and the draft. After the war, teams started to look for sponsors since the company no longer sponsored a team. The 1960 Vintondale team was sponsored by the VFW.

On the 1927–1928 boys' varsity basketball team are George Lybarger, Roy Kuchenbrod, Lloyd Williams, Russell Kuchenbrod, and Jack Frazier. Standing are Bruce Lybarger, George Hozik, Michael Hozik, Edward Nevy, Geno Avali, Clarence Huey, Richard Benetti, Jack Burgan, William Jendrick and Mario Biancotti. Burgan moved to Ferndale in his junior year and became a newspaperman and published novelist. Two of his books are about Vintondale. He was killed in a plane crash in California in 1947. (Courtesy of Agnes Huth Dusza.)

This championship girls' basketball team is from the early 1930s. Pictured in this Deck Lane Studio photograph, from left to right are (first row) Isabel Jendrick, Anne Hrabar, Olga Kanich, Mary Skvarcek, K. Biancotti and Alice Sileck; (second row) Mary Suprak, Ailene Lynch, Irene Davali, Vera Mae Evans, Lynette Daly, Aileen Huth, and Elizabeth Neggie; (third row) Sue Sileck, Margaret Morris, Virginia Daly, Erdene Lynch, Mary Hozik, and Anna Balog. (Courtesy of Charles Sago.)

Company-sponsored baseball teams were the norm in the mining towns of western Pennsylvania. In Vintondale, the team shirts read Vintondale YMCA, but most likely the sponsor was the Vinton Colliery Company. This early team photograph dates from around 1906. John Huth (lower right) is the only identified ballplayer in the photograph. His bat and glove are still in the possession of the family. (Courtesy of the Julius Morey collection.)

This 1932 baseball team would still have been under Vinton Colliery Company sponsorship. The bat boys in the front are James Samitore (left) and Andrew "Copper" Grosik. From left to right are (first row) Frederick Michelbacher, Carl Michelbacher, Charles Butala, John Risko, Andrew Markus, Joseph Wojtowicz, and Stephen Kish; (second row) Freland Scaife, Michael Grosik, Andrew Beres, Joseph Lonetti, William Cooke, and Michael Kerekish. (Courtesy of Aileen Ure and Fred Michelbacher.)

Carl Michelbacher is up to bat. Note the homemade backstop. This photograph may have been taken in Nanty Glo or Portage. (Courtesy of Aileen Ure and Fred Michelbacher.)

After World War II, enthusiasm for baseball waned in Vintondale. The leagues were now sponsored by service clubs and businesses. This team, sponsored by the VFW, played a game on the baseball field in Wehrum in 1960. From left to right are (first row) coach Paul Pytash with his daughter Chrissy, Rodney Peterson, Joseph Gresko, and John Shestak; (second row) Edward Wojtowicz, Robert Garvis, Andrew Marcus, Ronald Toth, John Antol, Charles (Chuck) Holupka, Maurice Dick, Raymond Hunter, and Stephen Hegedus. (Courtesy of Claire Sebulsky.)

Before unionization, the Vinton Colliery Company controlled the recreational activities in Vintondale by owning the movie theater, organizing the holiday picnics, and bringing in carnivals. After 1933, these were taken over by the union. One popular event was drinking beer through baby bottle nipples. (Courtesy of Julius Morey collection.)

This beer drinking contest was held on Main Street in front of Cresswell Electric and drew large crowds in 1945. The post office was in the duplex in the background. The building at the extreme left was Krumbine's Undertaking and Paint Store. (Courtesy of Julius Morey collection.)

Swimming was relegated to local streams and farm ponds. Many hiked to "Big Ducky" on the north branch of the Blacklick Creek where they swam in polluted water. Rock and sod dams could be found above the houses on Shuman and Bracken Runs. Wehrum Dam, abandoned when Wehrum shut down, was a big lure to youngsters in spite of the three-mile hike to reach it. (Courtesy of Aileen Ure and Fred Michelbacher.)

Two outings turned tragic as William Kerezsi of Nanty Glo drowned June 10, 1943, and James Balest, age 14, drowned there in 1944. The spillway of the dam was eroding in the 1940s and washed out in the 1977 flood. The breast of the Wehrum Dam is still standing today. (Courtesy of Aileen Ure and Fred Michelbacher.)

Nine

WORLD WAR II

When World War II was declared, the citizens of Vintondale stepped forward and honorably served in the military or on the home front. In Vintondale alone, over 340 men and women volunteered or were drafted into the service. One of the first people to head out was John "Bones" Dusza, but he saw no overseas action. Dusza was assigned to run a canteen at a camp in Virginia. In many families, several children were in the service. Three of Jack Huth's daughters, Aileen, Margaret, and Christine, served in the navy and the army. The Kozar family suffered the unthinkable loss of two sons, Michael and John, and Tom Whinnie spent over a month in a Nazi prisoner-of-war camp. At home, everyone had to sign up for ration books, conserve metals, endure meatless and wheatless days, grow victory gardens and buy U.S. savings bonds. The names of all who have served have been memorialized at the VFW.

Three of Mable and John Huth's seven daughters enlisted in the armed services. From left to right are Carol; Jean; Christine, an ensign in the navy; Claire "Tood" James; Margaret, a second lieutenant in the U.S. Army Nurse Corps; Aileen Michelbacher; and Agnes Dusza. Aileen enlisted in the Women's Army Corps shortly after the photograph was taken and followed her husband, Carl Michelbacher, into the army. Carl was stationed in Australia. (Courtesy of the Huth family collection.)

Aileen served as a clerk in Australia and the Philippines. She is seen here riding a water buffalo. Following the war, she used the GI Bill to attend nursing school in Philadelphia. (Courtesy of the Huth family collection.)

Joseph Wojtowicz, son of Andrew and Stella Wojtowicz, was killed in France in 1944. This photograph was taken when he was home on leave in June 1942. (Courtesy of Estelle Wojtowicz.)

George Larish, son of George Larish and Anna Larish Sermeg, was killed on June 10, 1944. He was a paratrooper in the 101st Airborne. (Courtesy of Dr. Boyd Brandon.)

This photograph of George Leleck was approved by the naval censor. (Courtesy of the Huth family collection.)

Carl Michelbacher served in the U.S. Army in the Pacific. This photograph was taken in June 1942. (Courtesy of Aileen Ure and Fred Michelbacher.)

Home on leave were Eugene Gasser (left) and Richard "Dick" Sebulsky (second from left). Also in the photograph, from left to right, are John Smith, William Roberts, James Roberts, and Aileen Cresswell. (Courtesy of Aileen Ure and Fred Michelbacher.)

Thomas Whinnie (left) served in the U.S. Army and was captured near Cologne on February 28, 1945. He spent 33 days in a Nazi prisoner-of-war camp and months in army hospitals recuperating from his ordeal. (Courtesy of the Huth family collection.)

1944

Commencement Exercises

Class Roll

x Asti Arthur	Eleanor Hasen
x George Balich	x Charles Holupka
x Mike Balog	Bernard McConnell
Mario Bisnucci	x Joseph Minarovich
x John Borczik	Gloria Risko
Charles Brazil	x William Rosner
Betty Brazil	Ann Shestak
Ethel Beres	Lillian Simoneini
Erma Cassol	x Steve Sofko
Gayle Findley	Julia Telesko
x Eli Ugljesa	

x Serving in the Armed Forces

BECKLEY PRINT, PORTAGE, PA.

Vintondale High School
Monday Evening, May Twenty-Ninth
Eight O'clock   *Vintondale State Theatre*

The 1944 commencement exercises of Vintondale High School demonstrates the impact of the war not only on the school but also on the whole community. Nine out of 21 members of the class were in the service. (Courtesy of Jean Huth Hammer.)

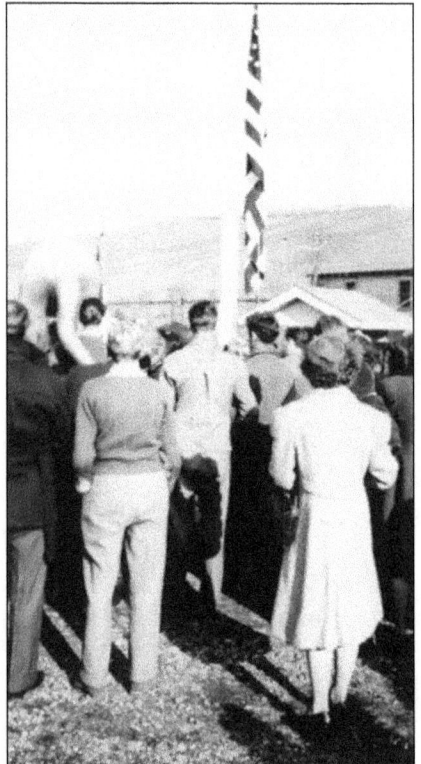

In 1946, the war memorial at the head of Main Street was refurbished and rededicated. The stonework was done by Roberto Ugoletti of Dilltown. (Courtesy of Charles Sago.)

114

Ten

FAMILIES

Many of Vintondale's first families, such as Samuel Williams's, came from the surrounding farms. The Wrays arrived from the Homer City area. Others were involved in the lumbering or railroad industry. The coal mines attracted skilled workers from the hard coal region like the Roberts, Huth, and Daly families. Some had worked at other Claghorn mines like the Hampsons and the Blewitts. As Vintondale grew, so did the need for labor, and more and more immigrants began to call Vintondale home permanently. Michael Petrilla arrived in the late 1890s, and his descendents still reside here. Each resident, past or present, has a unique story to tell about his or her family's Vintondale experience.

Meri and John Morey Sr. and their family emigrated from Hungary and settled in Pine Hill, Somerset County. They moved to Vintondale in 1909 and lived in the double house at the foot of Second Street. There Meri ran a boardinghouse and John Sr. was a miner. A son, Julius, was born in the house in 1912 and died there in 2002. Seen here, from left to right, are John Jr., Meri, Elizabeth, John Sr., and Stephen. (Courtesy of the Julius Morey collection.)

Andrew Beres and Julia Zoltanski were married in September 1938 at the Hungarian Reformed Church. The wedding reception was held at the company social hall on Plank Road. The flower girl on the left is Charlotte Zoltanski. The ring bearer is Nicholas "Mickey" Farkas. From left to right are (first row) Esther Molnar, Isabel George, Margaret Fulerki, Betty Orban, Julia Beres, Michael Andrew Beres, Mary Beres, Margaret Kelly, Elizabeth Beres, Helen Farkas, and Helen Farkas; (second row) Stephen Joth, Nicholas Hollis, George Grosik, Carl Michelbacher, John Beres, Elizabeth Farkas, Gabriel Joth, John Harnots, Stephen Antol, Peter Szabo, and Mike Farkas.

116

John and Meri Morey celebrated their 50th wedding anniversary in the late 1940s with a family dinner in their yard. Standing behind the Moreys are their son John Jr. (left) and a boarder, Joseph Silagyi. John Jr. had a gypsy orchestra that played for weddings and the grape dances that were held at the social hall in the fall. (Courtesy of the Julius Morey collection.)

Dancing the *czardas*, the Hungarian national dance, was part of the celebration. From left to right, Emma and Steve Morey, Elizabeth and John Rabel, and Martha and Julius Morey are dancing to the gypsy music of John Jr. and Silagyi. (Courtesy of the Julius Morey collection.)

John Paney (also spelled Panyi), nicknamed "Paney Basci," was one of the numerous Vintondale bachelors who had emigrated from Austria-Hungary. He boarded with Helen Firko. Here he is seen holding Diane Dusza around 1945. (Courtesy of Diane Dusza.)

The Pisaneschi family posed for this photograph around 1938. Seen from left to right are Merle, Arthur, Albert, Josephine, Alfred, and Hugh. (Courtesy of Albert Pisaneschi.)

John Bossolo, father of Josephine Pisaneschi, lived with his daughter for many years. He could be seen walking the Dinkey Track daily with his hands clasped behind his back. (Courtesy of Albert Pisaneschi.)

Hunting was and still is an important pastime in Vintondale. Seen here are, from left to right, (first row) unidentified and Billy Toth; (second row) Baloz Toth, William Toth, and Lloyd Williams. The photograph was taken by Thomas Kasper in 1945 and was not developed until 1998. (Courtesy of Joanne Kasper Vasilko.)

Around 1905, residents gathered near No. 3 mine for a photograph. Pictured are, from left to right, (first row) Walter Treaster, Grace Treaster, Cloyd Hoffman, and Thomas Hoffman holding Percy Hoffman; (second row) Jennie Kempher, Doyle Hoffman, and Russell Hoffman; (standing) Annie Hoffman Treaster holding Hazel, Rhett Treaster Kempher holding Warren, Lizzie Hoffman, Mable Hampson, and Eula Hampson. (Courtesy of Aileen Ure and Fred Michelbacher.)

About 50 years later, the Hampson sisters celebrated Mable's birthday. Both sisters had married Vinton Colliery Company officials. Jean Huth Hammer and her daughter Brenda hosted John Huth, Louis Burr, Eula Burr, and Mable Huth at the Hammer home in Johnstown. (Courtesy of Jean Huth Hammer.)

Visiting the Huth residence in the 1930s, from left to right, are Isabel Jendrick, Emma Jane Daly, Betty Daly, and William Jendrick with George Larish kneeling. (Courtesy of the Huth family collection.)

Carl Michelbacher and his mother, Ada, pose on the back porch of their home on Third Street. (Courtesy of Aileen Ure and Fred Michelbacher.)

Dr. James MacFarlane arrived as the Vinton Colliery Company doctor in 1912 and remained until 1936 when the union chose its own physician. MacFarlane opened a practice in Indiana, Pennsylvania, and died there in 1937. Before he left Vintondale, his office burned to the ground on March 12, 1936. (Courtesy of James MacFarlane.)

Alice Jose MacFarlane, MacFarlane's wife, hailed from the Clearfield County town of LaJose. After her husband's death, she resided in Indiana, Pennsylvania, until her death in 1976. (Courtesy of Aileen Ure and Fred Michelbacher.)

In 1937, Dr. Philip Ashman replaced
Dr. Jerome Cohen as the town doctor.
D. Cohen, the replacement for
Dr. MacFarlane, left to study ophthalmology.
Ashman joined the armed services in 1940.
He and his wife Mary had two children,
Jerome and Fay. Ashman returned to
Johnstown after World War II and was
instrumental in starting the Hiram G.
Andrews Rehabilitation Center. (Courtesy
of Margaret Huth Schmidt.)

In 1981, three longtime residents of Vintondale attended the annual homecoming. From left to right, Sara Williams George, daughter of Samuel Williams and wife of Del George, helped run George's Economy Store; Harry Ling was the Prudential Insurance Company agent in Vintondale; and Cora Bracken Roberts, wife of Roy Roberts, was a telephone operator in the Vinton Colliery Company office during the early 1920s. (Courtesy of Jean Huth Hammer.)

Gabriel "Gig" Hubner, who worked on the No. 6 tipple, was also the town's shoemaker. He took over as shoemaker when his father, Steve, retired. In this 1980 photograph, Gig just received two loaves of bakery bread that Steve Dusza had delivered. (Courtesy of the Dusza collection.)

Joseph Pioli arrived from Italy in 1922 and went to work at the Nevy brothers' store. His brother Frank, married to Paulina Nevy, also worked there. Joe remained at the store until it was sold in the late 1960s. Seated on Joe's lap is his wife, Jennie. (Courtesy of Raymond Pioli.)

William "Bill" McKeel lived on Rexis Hill and was the janitor at the First Baptist church. (Courtesy of Harold Swanson.)

This winter scene was shot in the Huth family's yard around 1940. From left to right are Frank Brandon, Gordon Whinnie, William Sebulsky, Carol Huth, and William Roberts. (Courtesy of the John Huth collection.)

Charles and Naydeen Rosner Leleck and their daughter Paula were paying a visit to the Huth home around 1952. (Courtesy of Aileen Ure and Fred Michelbacher.)

The Thomas Wray family was one of the first families to permanently settle in Vintondale. Seen in this photograph, from left to right, are family members James, William, and Oscar "Pete." A fourth brother, Frank, died in 1966. Several members of the family still live in Vintondale. (Courtesy of Mary Ellen Wray Pytash.)

This photograph of Joanne Kasper Vasilko, daughter of Thomas and Helena Kasper, was taken around 1944 and not processed until 1998.

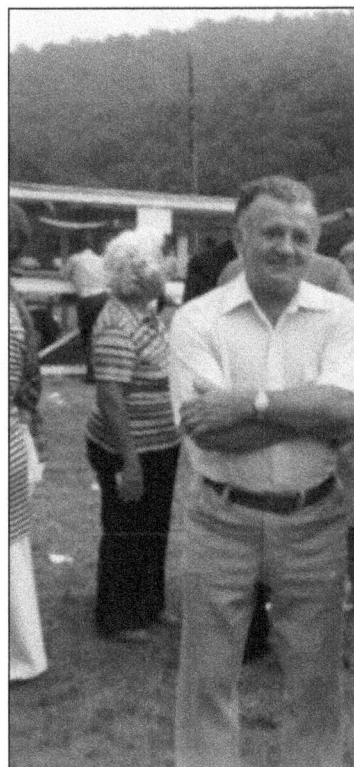

Stephen Oblackovich, mayor of Vintondale and Cambria County clerk of courts, is seen here at the Vintondale homecoming around 1981. Oblackovich had been the main target of the "Friend of a Friend" terror campaign in 1980 and 1981.

Visit us at
arcadiapublishing.com

....

www.ingramcontent.com/pod-product-compliance
Lightning Source LLC
Chambersburg PA
CBHW050607110426
42813CB00008B/2480